Ace Your Interview
Proven Techniques For Job Success
Tanya Abbey

First edition published in 2025 by Tanya Abbey under RecruitCorpGroup Pty Ltd

© Tanya Abbey 2025. All rights reserved.

No part of this publication may be reproduced, stored in a retrieval system, transmitted, or shared in any form or by any means—electronic, mechanical, photocopying, recording, or otherwise—without prior written permission of the publisher, except for brief quotations used for the purposes of review, reference, or educational instruction.

To request permission, please contact: pr@recruitcorp.com.au

This publication may be available in various formats, including print-on-demand and digital editions. Some supplementary content referenced in the print edition may not be included in all formats.

The right of the author to be identified as the creator of this work has been asserted under the Copyright Act 1968 (Cth), as amended.

All trademarks, product names, and company names mentioned in this book are the property of their respective owners and do not imply endorsement.

This book is catalogued and preserved in the collections of the National Library of Australia and the State Library of Queensland.

Contents

Praise For Author   1

Dedication   3

Acknowledgements   4

Epigraph   5

Preface   6

1. An Introduction   8
2. Setting the Stage   17
3. Preparing for the Interview   28
4. Understanding the Company   38
5. Overcoming Interview Anxiety   55
6. The Power of Non-Verbal Communication   68
7. Mastering Common Interview Questions   77
8. Mastering Behavioural and Situational Questions   89
9. Asking Questions in Job Interviews   95
10. Mastering Virtual Interviews   104
11. Adapting to Different and Challenging Interview Types   111

12.	Second Interview Strategies	125
13.	The 90-Day Plan	133
14.	Tips for Specific Industries	141
15.	Leveraging Social Media and Online Presence	149
16.	Networking and References	156
17.	Salary Negotiation Strategies	166
18.	Follow-Up After the Interview	181
19.	Shikha's Story	188
20.	Final Thoughts	191
Resources and Tools for Success		199
Afterword		228
About the Author		229
Also by Tanya Abbey		231

Praise For Author

Words from the People Who Know Her Best

"To the days, nights, weekends, hours, heart, and soul that you poured into this project—I couldn't be more proud of you! This book is a chance to reach those who won't have the opportunity to meet you. For that, I'm in awe." – Korey

"I still remember the first podcast I heard of yours, from years ago when you mentioned hiring for cultural enrichment — not fit — that stuck with me and I think about it often when hiring. The parts of your drafts showed me how personal this book is for you. And to put out your own stories — very inspiring. Really proud of you." – Nick

"This is a much-needed book—not just for those preparing for interviews, but also for emerging leaders and hiring managers. Hurry up and send me an invoice — I want 50 to start." – Timberland

"Writing a book is a major achievement — and doing so while raising two boys and building and leading a successful recruitment business is even more inspiring. This book isn't just a reflection of your journey; it's a valuable resource that will impact candidates when they need it most, recruiters, and businesses alike. Here's to this new chapter of influence and growth. Proud of you!" – Christie

"Tan's ability to break down what hiring managers are really looking for—and how to present your value—makes this more than just an interview guide. It's a confidence builder." – Client

"The layout is simple, relatable, and empowering. It's like having a coach, a cheerleader, and a practical roadmap all in one." – Client

"It made me feel confident that no matter who you are, what stage of your career you're in, or why you're job-hunting, there are simple ways to achieve your desired outcome. It also made me feel something I haven't felt in a while — hope." – Mentee

Dedication

To my sons, Manny and Panos, who always ask me how my day was, even though they think it consists of bougie lunches, endless phone calls, and spontaneous karaoke between meetings.
You have taught me that each step, no matter how little, is a step forward.
Thank you, my miracle children

Acknowledgements

This book is a reflection of the many incredible people who have shaped my journey, and I am deeply grateful for their support, encouragement, and wisdom. To my tribe—your unwavering support, energy, and belief in me have been my foundation. You've lifted me up during the challenging moments, celebrated every win alongside me, and held me accountable to my own goals. Your presence in my life is invaluable, and I am endlessly grateful. To the countless professionals I have interviewed over the years—thank you for sharing your stories, experiences, and aspirations with me. Each conversation has reinforced my passion for helping people navigate their career journeys with confidence and purpose. I hope this book serves as a resource that empowers you to take control of your own path, make informed decisions, and step into every interview with clarity and self-assurance.

And to everyone who has ever encouraged, challenged, or inspired me—thank you. Whether through a conversation, a lesson, or a shared experience, you have helped shape the insights and strategies within these pages.

This book is for you.

Epigraph

To actively seek out and listen to the stories of others, gaining wisdom from each individual I engage with, and leaving our encounter by imparting knowledge, a supportive word, or tools they can use to apply to their own development.

This is my purpose.

- Tanya Abbey

Preface

At some point in your life—whether by choice or necessity—you will find yourself looking for a new job. The market is constantly evolving, and the ability to adapt, learn, and embrace change is key to long-term career success. Those who take control of their career growth are the ones who seize the best opportunities.

That's why I wrote *Ace Your Interview: Proven Techniques for Job Success*. Whether you're entering the workforce, pivoting careers, or striving for a promotion, this book will equip you with the tools to navigate interviews with clarity, confidence, and control.

Having conducted over 15,000 interviews and placed more than 5,000 candidates, I've seen firsthand what separates successful candidates from those who struggle. Many people underestimate their ability to steer an interview—they assume they're there just to answer questions. The truth is, the best candidates guide the conversation, handle challenges confidently, and leave a lasting impression.

This book isn't about memorised scripts, gimmicks, or one-size-fits-all advice. It's about developing a structured, adaptable approach that allows you to prepare strategically while sounding natural and authentic. You'll learn how to sell yourself effectively without overselling, highlight your strengths with genuine confidence, and adapt to any interview scenario without sounding rehearsed.

Handling tough questions with composure, addressing gaps or challenges openly, and positioning yourself as the best choice for the role are all skills you'll master. You'll discover how to align your strengths with an employer's needs, communicate your unique value, and demonstrate not just your qualifications, but also your mindset and approach.

Finally, we'll cover what happens after the first interview: how to navigate second interviews, salary discussions, and follow-ups with professionalism and purpose. Understanding these stages is just as crucial as the interview itself in securing the right role.

This isn't just about getting hired—it's about making the right career move for your future. By understanding how to position yourself effectively, you can turn any interview into an opportunity to advance your career.

You will find your first, next, or forever job—and I will help you.

Chapter One
An Introduction

This chapter introduces my personal journey into recruitment, beginning with my very first interview experience. It highlights the lessons I learned, the challenges I faced, and how this experience shaped my approach to interviews and recruitment. By sharing this story, I aim to provide insight into the realities of the interview process, the importance of preparation, and the key takeaways that can help job seekers feel more confident and in control.

Key Points:

- Your first interview sets the stage for how you approach job opportunities.

- Preparation is crucial, but unexpected challenges will arise.

- Understanding the employer's perspective can help you navigate interviews more effectively.

- Every interview—good or bad—teaches valuable lessons that can shape your career.

- Confidence and adaptability are just as important as skills and experience.

My First Interview Experience

My first interview experience marked the beginning of my journey into recruitment, and I reflect on it often when putting myself in a job seeker's shoes. Securing an interview with a well-known recruitment firm, I think back to this event eighteen years ago and revisit the version of myself then.

I had no degree in human resources. No experience in HR, recruitment or formal business-to-business sales. My only sales experience came from telco phone sales (who remembers AAPT?!). Still, I set my sights on a career in the recruitment industry. A friend in my network sent me the job advertisement, and after a brief telephone interview with one of the recruitment administrators, I was scheduled to meet the manager at 9 a.m. the following Monday. The business unit, salary and job description remained undisclosed, prompting me to make a mental note to inquire about them on the day.

From my research, I knew the company was quite corporate, so I searched for the cheapest but most professional suit and new heels, totalling $350 - a significant dent in my meagre savings. This was twenty years ago so this wasn't a cheap outfit, especially by today's standards. Despite the stress and guilt of taking the morning off work for the interview, I was optimistic. Even back then, ever the optimist, I truly believed I'd impress the interviewer.

The night before, I called my friends and my mum to discuss my attire, the questions I would ask, how to shake hands, and how I should present myself. The advice? Be eager, but not desperate. Be mindful, but don't overthink.

On the morning of the interview, I took two buses to make sure I arrived early. But (and this is very typical of me), as I was stepping off the bus, I ripped my stocking on the door—a less-than-ideal start. I searched for a nearby café to change out of my stockings, but there wasn't one close to the interview location. For those familiar with Brisbane CBD, my bus stop was on the corner of Creek and Eagle, and back then, there wasn't much there besides a café packed with stressed-out lawyer and accounting grads and very cracked sidewalks that my new heels got stuck in as I crossed the road to the building where my interview was held.

I snuck into the lift amidst the crowd of suited-up young professionals, all exuding confidence I felt I didn't have, and I was already feeling a bit sweaty and agitated. When I reached the floor, I quickly walked to the restroom, covering my ripped stocking with my handbag, attempting to be incognito. Stockings were part of the dress code, so I hoped the interviewers would have a sense of humour about it if it came up.

After fixing my makeup, rubbing moisturiser on my legs, and stashing my stockings in my handbag (because what if they saw them in the bin?!), I walked through the front reception doors and told the receptionist my name with a big smile. She looked at me balefully, didn't smile back, but directed me to one of the couches and told me to wait for the interviewer.

I hadn't brought water or a notebook with me, so I sat there with a parched mouth, trying to memorise my questions and not feel nervous. I remember how sweaty my hands were, and I couldn't cross my legs because the seats were unusually low. So I just sat awkwardly, listening to the receptionist answering the phone in clipped, short tones, transferring potential clients and candidates on the switchboard, her long nails tapping, almost as though she was irritated that she had to work.

I waited in the reception area for 45 minutes before being shown to a boardroom, where I sat for another 30 minutes before the interviewer finally arrived. The manager of the department walked in with a disinterested, bored look on her face and placed a piece of paper face down on the table alongside her notebook and pen. Looking at me, she sighed and said, "So, what do you know about recruitment?"

My mind scrambled, I had rehearsed this response over and over and I still went blank. I responded, "Recruitment is a professional service provided by experienced recruitment companies to their clients to help them find staff for their jobs. It's also to help people find a job." That's essentially what recruitment is, but my answer came out stilted, scripted, and unsure.

She then peppered me with questions about my sales experience—what I currently did, how many times I hit my sales target, and the kinds of people I dealt with—all with a passive expression on her face. With each answer, she wrote in her notebook, putting lines under certain things while tapping her fingernail on the table.

It really threw me off—the disinterest, the long waits, the way she barely acknowledged my responses. I felt like I was failing, but I wasn't sure how or why. I worried about being late for my current role, how to answer these questions correctly, and when was a good time to ask my own.

After 20 minutes of answering questions, she turned over the piece of paper and pushed it towards me. It was the job description for a Junior Recruitment Administrator/Coordinator, not a Recruitment Consultant, outlining the duties, KPIs, and skills needed for the role. The salary was also $5,000 less than my current salary ($33,000 plus superannuation)—legal, but right on the minimum wage.

I tentatively asked her if there was a miscommunication, as I was looking for a Recruitment Consultant role and hoping for a salary that matched my expectations, skills, and experience. She told me that based on the company's needs and my résumé, this was the only role they were willing to offer.

I hadn't had the chance to learn about the team, ask my questions, discuss my strengths, or state my long-term goals, nor was I given the opportunity to review the position description prior to the job interview. I felt underprepared but also a bit blindsided by the role change. I left the interview feeling uncertain about the role, whether I wanted to work there, what the next steps were, and what I could have done to regain some sort of control in the interview.

After three more interviews (yes, three) with some of the other consultants who asked me the same kind of questions, then a psychological profile test along with a basic computer test, I was successful in the position. Despite the lengthy process, extra outfit purchases and time off work, I took the role happily, to get a foot in the door to a career I was passionate about.

Shortly after an uncomfortable but lesson-filled "trial by fire" experience under that manager, I was taken on by another manager in another department as a Recruitment Consultant within three months. This new manager became the cornerstone of my commitment to conducting recruitment authentically and ethically.

That first experience—along with many others, though thankfully less intimidating—became the driving force behind my dedication to helping candidates prepare. It's why I've spent countless hours guiding job seekers, coaching clients on authentic interviewing, and ultimately, writing this book for you.

Welcome to Ace Your Interview: Proven Techniques for Job Success

This book draws on nearly two decades of recruitment experience—insights shaped from the moment I stepped into my very first interview. I know how daunting and frustrating interviews can feel, but with the right preparation, they become powerful opportunities to take control of your career.

Throughout my career, I've seen firsthand the challenges candidates face and the strategies that set successful applicants apart. Whether you're a seasoned professional, a graduate entering the workforce, or someone re-entering the job market, this book will equip you with the tools, insights, and confidence to navigate interviews with clarity and purpose.

In today's market, securing a role isn't just about ticking boxes. Interviews often last thirty to sixty minutes—just a short window to build rapport, showcase your experience, and determine whether the opportunity aligns with your goals. Every moment counts.

The job search itself signals transition—whether you're moving from study to work, pivoting careers, or stepping into leadership. Strategic planning and adaptability are critical advantages in today's evolving landscape. Candidates who understand market trends, employer expectations, and how to position their value have a distinct edge.

Yet interviews remain one of the most misunderstood and underprepared-for stages of job hunting. Many candidates believe experience alone will carry them through. In reality, it's preparation—thoughtful, strategic, and authentic—that transforms an interview from a test into a genuine opportunity to demonstrate your value.

Why Interviews Matter for Employers Too

For employers, hiring is a high-stakes decision. A bad hire doesn't just cost time—it can impact revenue, team morale, and even client relationships. Studies show that replacing a poor hire can cost businesses hundreds of thousands of dollars when factoring in lost productivity, training expenses, and the ripple effect on existing employees.

Smaller businesses feel these impacts even more acutely. A recruitment misstep could mean wasted investment in new equipment, disrupted workflows, and additional training expenses. A well-structured, thoughtful hiring process is critical—not just for bringing in the right people, but for long-term retention and team cohesion.

The Role of Recruiters in Your Success

Recruitment isn't just about matching job seekers with roles—it's about positioning candidates to thrive. A good recruiter serves as both a coach and an advocate, ensuring candidates are prepared for more than just answering questions. We provide insight into employer expectations, hiring trends, and even the unwritten rules of job interviews.

However, not all recruiters operate with the same level of diligence. Many transactional recruiters focus on volume, pushing candidates into as many roles as possible, often at the expense of fit. This book goes beyond that approach, offering tailored guidance to help you not only secure a job but choose the right one.

The Digital Shift in Recruitment

The way people search for jobs has evolved. The days of walking into an office and handing over a résumé are long gone. Today, professional networking sites, digital applications, and AI-driven platforms dominate the hiring landscape. While job hunting has become more accessible, it's also brought new challenges—your online presence must now align with your professional aspirations just as much as your interview performance does.

With hiring managers facing tighter timeframes, candidates must be deliberate in how they present themselves. Employers aren't just scanning qualifications; they want to understand your story, your impact, and what sets you apart. Standing out begins long before you walk into the room. To truly ace an interview, it's important to understand what happens behind the scenes. Imagine a business owner receiving a resignation with just two weeks' notice. Suddenly, they're juggling their regular workload while scrambling to fill a critical gap.

The recruitment process unfolds in multiple stages: reviewing applications, conducting interviews, arranging second rounds, testing skills, checking references, and finalising offers. Each step demands time, resources, and focus. The easier you make this process—by being prepared, clear about your strengths, and aligned with the company's needs—the stronger your candidacy becomes.

One of the biggest mistakes candidates make is assuming interviews are one-sided. In reality, they're a two-way process. Companies are assessing your suitability—but you should also be evaluating whether their leadership, culture, and future opportunities align with your career goals.

When you understand a company's challenges, growth opportunities, and team dynamics, you position yourself as a solution—not just another applicant. Employers aren't just looking for someone who can do the job; they want someone who will contribute meaningfully.

What You'll Learn in This Book

Interviews can feel overwhelming, but they don't have to be. In this book, you'll learn how to:

- Strategically prepare without sounding rehearsed.

- Sell yourself authentically, highlighting your strengths without overselling.

- Handle tough or unexpected questions with composure.

- Understand what hiring managers are really looking for—and position yourself as the best choice.

- Master second interviews, salary discussions, and follow-up strategies to secure the right offer.

These are the exact techniques I've used to prepare thousands of candidates across industries and career stages. Whether you're applying for a promotion, re-entering the workforce, or chasing your first role, this book will guide you step-by-step to success.

Before we dive into specific strategies and question types, it's important to take a step back and look at the bigger picture. What actually happens behind the scenes of the interview process? How do companies make decisions, and why does the experience vary so much from one organisation to the next?

Chapter Two
Setting the Stage
Understanding Interview Dynamics

The recruitment process plays a pivotal role in shaping career opportunities and business growth. Ideally, it should be a well-organised and transparent system, providing both candidates and employers with the clarity needed to make informed decisions. However, many businesses lack a structured approach, leading to inefficiencies, miscommunication, and missed opportunities.

This chapter explores the dynamics of the recruitment and interview process—how it should work, the common challenges businesses and candidates face, and the strategies you can use to navigate these challenges effectively.

Key Points:

- The ideal recruitment process vs. real-world recruitment challenges

- The role of interviews in setting expectations and building rapport

- Why structured recruitment processes matter for both candidates and employers

- How candidates can guide and optimise their interview experience

- The importance of transparency, preparation, and active participation

The Ideal Recruitment Process vs. Reality

In an ideal world, recruitment would be seamless. Companies would provide clear, detailed information upfront—covering job responsibilities, team structure, company culture, and opportunities for growth. Position descriptions would be comprehensive, giving candidates a full and realistic picture of what to expect. The interview itself would be a structured, two-way conversation where both parties assess alignment. Candidates would come in well-informed, and employers would follow a clear, consistent process for evaluation. The entire experience would be professional, efficient, and mutually beneficial.

The Reality of Recruitment in Many Businesses

However, the reality is often very different. Many businesses, particularly small to medium-sized enterprises (SMEs), do not have a structured recruitment process in place. Instead, hiring is handled by individuals who have other primary responsibilities—such as department managers, operations leads, or even business owners. These individuals may lack the time, expertise, or resources to conduct a thorough hiring process.

This often leads to:

- Lack of structure in the hiring process – Candidates are left to figure things out for themselves, leading to uncertainty.

- Poorly defined job roles or expectations – Position descriptions are vague or outdated, causing confusion about the role's actual responsibilities.

- Rushed decision-making due to time constraints – Employers may hire reactively rather than strategically, leading to poor hiring choices.

- Limited onboarding processes – New hires may not receive the proper training or resources to integrate successfully.

Without a structured hiring process, both employers and candidates face challenges. Candidates are left to fill in the gaps, researching a company on their own and navigating unclear expectations. Meanwhile, companies risk missing out on top talent due to disorganised processes, delayed decision-making, or a lack of transparency.

A well-conducted interview isn't just about answering questions—it's a two-way conversation. It's an opportunity to assess alignment, set expectations, and build rapport. Transparency is key—not just in terms of job responsibilities, but also in highlighting what both parties bring to the table, including skills, values, and long-term potential.

Understanding these challenges is the first step toward navigating them effectively. Whether you're a candidate preparing for an interview or a business aiming to improve hiring, recognising the common pitfalls can help you approach the process more strategically. The recruitment process isn't just about filling a vacancy—it's about ensuring the right fit for both the company and the candidate, setting the stage for long-term success.

What a Strong Recruitment Process and Interview Structure Looks Like

The following two pages outline a best-practice recruitment process and interview structure. While not every company will follow this to the letter, it serves as a benchmark for what you should expect—or what you should be prepared to prompt for.

Too often, candidates walk into interviews without a clear sense of the bigger picture. They're focused on *this one interview*—not realising that how they prepare, follow up, and engage at every stage of the process can influence the outcome just as much as what's said in the room.

Understanding the full recruitment lifecycle—from the moment a job is advertised to the final offer—can help you anticipate what's coming next. It also gives you a framework to ask the right questions, read between the lines, and show up with clarity and confidence at every stage.

These next two pages will walk you through that process visually, giving you a snapshot of how great recruitment should look when it's done well.

> ***Reflection Prompt:*** Before you turn the page, take a moment to reflect on the most recent interview you were part of—whether as a candidate, hiring manager, or observer. What steps were handled well? What was missing, rushed, or unclear? Were you given enough information to prepare, feel confident, and understand the expectations? If not, how did that shape your overall impression of the experience—and would you approach anything differently next time?

Interview Process

STAGE ONE
Introductions between interviewer/s and candidate
Overview of interviewer roles
Ice-breaker and rapport building

STAGE TWO
Company intro, history and growth
Role overview
Role's place in the team
Candidate's experience, qualifications and key highlights

STAGE THREE
Career history and reasons for changes
Addressing any gaps or concerns
Strengths, weaknesses, and transferable skills
Behavioural questions

STAGE FOUR
Candidate questions around training, salary, benefits, etc.
Inclusions like bonus or car allowance
Wrap-up and next steps
Timeline for hearing back

POST-INTERVIEW
Thank you email
Providing references and completed by the company
Receiving update and feedback within appropriate timeframe
Next steps if successful

Understanding Interview Structure: A Key to Confidence and Control

Understanding the structure of an interview allows you to shift from being a passive participant to an active, engaged professional in your job search. Clarity on how a well-run interview should unfold helps you identify when an interview is structured effectively versus when it lacks organisation. It also enables you to ask insightful questions that uncover valuable details about the role and company, spot red flags that indicate a poorly managed hiring process and guide the conversation in a way that highlights your experience and strengths.

A structured interview typically lasts between 45 to 60 minutes, providing enough time for a meaningful discussion about your qualifications, how they align with the role, and how you would fit into the company. Longer interviews are common for senior or technical positions. Those that last less than 30 minutes can signal one of two things: either the interviewer is highly efficient and knows exactly what they need, or the hiring process is rushed and disorganised.

If an interview feels too short or lacks depth, you can take initiative by steering the conversation toward key topics. Asking questions such as, "I'd love to hear more about the company culture and team dynamic—what does success look like in this role?" or "Could you tell me about the company's goals for the next six months and how this role contributes to them?" encourages the interviewer to provide more context beyond surface-level job details.

These types of questions help you gain a clearer understanding of the opportunity and whether it aligns with your career goals.

Taking an Active Role in the Interview

Even if the interviewer does not follow a structured process, you can subtly take control of the conversation by positioning yourself as an engaged and proactive candidate.

One way to do this is by initiating a balanced flow of discussion. A statement like, "Thank you for taking the time to meet with me today. I'd love to hear about the company, the team, and how this role fits into your broader objectives. Once you're ready, I'd be happy to share more about my background and how my experience aligns with this position," helps set the tone for the interview. It ensures the interviewer provides the necessary information upfront while giving you the opportunity to present yourself in the best possible way.

This approach achieves three important things. First, it sets the right tone—polite, professional, and proactive. Second, it invites the interviewer to offer insights before diving into questions, allowing you to tailor your responses effectively. Third, it positions you as an equal in the conversation, reinforcing that interviews are about mutual fit, not just an employer assessing a candidate.

Spotting Red Flags in the Hiring Process

Not every company has a well-designed recruitment process, and how an interview is conducted can reveal a lot about the organisation's internal operations. While each company approaches hiring differently, there are some warning signs that may indicate a lack of structure.

If the interviewer struggles to clearly define the role's responsibilities, it could mean the company has not taken the time to properly outline the position. A lack of discussion around career growth or professional development may signal that progression opportunities are limited. Frequent changes in interview details, last-minute scheduling shifts, or unclear communication can indicate poor internal coordination. If the interviewer is evasive about next steps or unclear about decision-making timelines, it may suggest that hiring priorities are unstructured or delayed. Another potential red flag is rapid-fire hiring—if you are offered the job on the spot without much discussion, it could point to high turnover, a desperate hiring need, or a lack of a thorough screening process.

Identifying these red flags does not necessarily mean you should walk away from an opportunity, but it does mean you should ask more questions and carefully evaluate whether the company aligns with your expectations and career aspirations.

First Impressions and Follow-Through

First impressions in an interview are a two-way street. It's not just about how you show up—it's also about how the company presents itself to you. A structured, well-organised interview should leave both sides with a sense of confidence about the opportunity and the process ahead.

As a candidate, the way you prepare and carry yourself speaks volumes. Arriving with a printed résumé, maintaining confident body language, engaging naturally, and closing with a simple, "Thank you for your time today—I appreciate the opportunity to learn more about the role," helps you leave a strong impression. These small, intentional moments reflect your professionalism and your respect for the process.

Equally, the employer's approach to the interview can offer valuable insight. A conversation that feels thoughtful, clear, and well-paced signals a company that values its people and has a deliberate hiring process. On the flip side, if things feel rushed or unclear, it may reflect deeper issues—like poor communication, lack of structure, or inconsistent leadership.

Understanding interview structure helps you stay proactive—even when the process isn't perfect. You'll know what questions to ask, like "What are the next steps?" or "Who else might I meet in the next stage?" These kinds of prompts show initiative while helping you clarify where things are headed.

If an interview lacks structure or starts to feel off track, don't be afraid to gently steer it. You could say: "I'd love to hear a bit more about the company, the team, and the role in your own words. Once you're ready, I'd be happy to share how my experience aligns."

This approach shows you're thoughtful and engaged—and ensures key topics are covered on both sides.

When preparing job seekers for interviews, I always emphasise the importance of first impressions. A confident handshake, strong eye contact, and genuine interest go a long way. Arriving with your notes or résumé reinforces your preparedness—and shows that you're engaged and ready to contribute meaningfully to the conversation.

The Power of Understanding Interview Structure

Understanding interview structure is not just about preparation—it is about empowerment. Knowing what to expect and how to navigate the process gives you control, even in high-pressure situations. It allows you to engage meaningfully, ask insightful questions, and ensure that the conversation covers all necessary aspects of the role and company. When you approach an interview with a clear understanding of how it should be conducted, you create opportunities to showcase your strengths while evaluating whether the role is the right fit for you.

In the next chapter, we will explore Preparing for an Interview—the critical first step in acing any recruitment process. We will look at how to research a company effectively, craft responses that highlight your strengths, and approach the interview with confidence. Preparation is the foundation of success, ensuring you present yourself as a well-informed, capable, and engaged candidate.

Chapter Three
Preparing for the Interview
Setting yourself up for success

Preparing for an interview is one of the most important parts of the job search journey. It's that critical next step after you've submitted your application or received a callback—and it's where many candidates either gain confidence or lose it entirely.

As part of our internal process, we always take time to 'prep' our candidates—usually the day before, or the day of the interview—regardless of how experienced they are. Why? Because even the best candidates get nervous.

A little extra preparation can help answer last-minute questions, boost confidence, and ensure they walk into the interview feeling grounded and ready. This chapter unpacks exactly how to do that. It also introduces an Interview Preparation overview, ensuring no crucial detail is overlooked. The overarching message is that preparation not only boosts confidence but also positions candidates to take control of their interview experience.

Key Points:
- Preparation Boosts Confidence – Researching the company, role, and interviewer helps candidates tailor responses and make a strong impression.

- Know the Interview Process – Understanding logistics, dress codes, and interviewer details prevents last-minute stress.

- Strategic Positioning – Aligning strengths with company goals helps steer the conversation and showcase value.

- Interview Preparation – An overview covering research, documentation, attire, and strategy ensures candidates are fully prepared.

This chapter explores the importance of thorough preparation before an interview, using the real-life experience of Shikha, a mentee of mine and a determined job seeker who faced challenges in securing a role despite her strong qualifications. Through her journey, we see how being open to learning, persistence, strategic preparation, and effective mentoring can lead to breakthrough moments in a competitive job market.

Shikha's Story: From Overlooked to Interview-Ready

Shikha is one of my recent mentees, and working with her was an incredibly rewarding experience. We connected twice a month through the Headspace Career Mentoring Program, which I've been part of for over two years and continue to support today. It's a wonderful program that matches young people with working professionals who volunteer their time to share insights, guidance, and real-world experience. Shikha was my second mentee, and our time together reminded me just how powerful this kind of support can be. Headspace is an Australian non-profit organisation dedicated to youth mental health, established by the Australian Government in 2006.

Originally from India, Shikha moved to Australia to complete a Master's in Molecular Biology. After graduating, she worked as a Lab Research Assistant at her university while actively applying for roles in her field, hoping to extend her visa or secure sponsorship. Despite her qualifications, the job search proved challenging — she applied for more than 80 roles over the course of a year, received limited responses, and was invited to just one interview with little to no feedback.

Throughout that period, Shikha worked in a fast-food outlet, volunteered, and dedicated her spare time to keeping up with scientific developments — reading case studies, reviewing breakthroughs, and maintaining her technical knowledge. Her resilience and work ethic were evident in everything she did.

By the time we began working together, her persistence, professionalism, and openness to learning were undeniable. She had made countless sacrifices — moving to Australia alone, travelling more than an hour each way to her hospitality job, volunteering, and continuing to pursue her professional goals. She was even willing to relocate interstate for the right opportunity.

One of my fondest memories from our first session was discovering our shared love of books. It became a recurring theme in our conversations. I still remember her reading *Doctor Zhivago* — one of my favourites and the inspiration behind my first name (my mum loved the film adaptation and changed the spelling to Tanya). We found so many synergies in our sessions beyond our mutual love of reading, which made our working relationship flow naturally and strengthened our collaboration.

Over the eight months we worked together, Shikha and I revised her résumé, tailored her applications, and developed strategies for reaching out directly to hiring managers to better understand their recruitment processes.

The Recruiter Gap: When Preparation Falls on the Candidate

Shikha is truly one of the most impressive individuals I've had the pleasure of mentoring. She approached every session with positivity, a deep willingness to learn, and a quiet confidence that grew stronger with each interaction. Even though she was diligent in her preparation, Shikha sometimes felt out of her depth when it came to interviews. She was determined to present her strengths authentically and make the most of any opportunity. Seeing her growth and commitment over our time together made every small win feel like a shared victory.

Throughout our mentoring relationship, we connected via video chats, phone calls, and emails. We refined her résumé and cover letters for different opportunities, discussed how to approach hiring managers, understood peak hiring seasons, and worked through strategies for reaching out via LinkedIn or responding to job adverts. We also focused heavily on follow-up strategies — requesting feedback, identifying hidden opportunities, and strengthening her responses over time. It was frustrating to see how often her applications went unacknowledged, despite her impressive credentials and proactive follow-ups. Unfortunately, disorganised hiring processes, unconscious bias, and rushed decisions still cause many talented candidates like Shikha to be overlooked.

But Shikha's experience also revealed a bigger gap in the hiring process—one that goes beyond résumés and preparation. Even the most capable, proactive candidates are often left in the dark, receiving little to no feedback after applying or interviewing. It's a reminder that hiring is a two-way street. While candidates carry the burden of preparation, employers and recruiters also have a responsibility to engage respectfully.

> **Call Out to Hiring Managers**
>
> *Don't ghost great candidates.*
>
> A simple follow-up, even if it's a "not this time," can leave a lasting positive impression—and supports candidate growth.
>
> *Before You Hit Send*
>
> Are you sending the same generic rejection to every applicant? Candidates like Shikha put in hours of preparation.
>
> You don't need to give full feedback—but a few tailored lines go a long way.
>
> *Feedback Isn't Optional*
>
> You might not realise it, but your silence could be costing you great talent. Respect the time, energy, and hope that goes into every application.

Shikha's story didn't end there—and neither did her growth.

In our second-to-last session, she shared the exciting news that she had secured an interview through a recruitment company for a role with their client. It was such a great moment for both of us—her hard work was finally paying off!

This was only her second job interview during our time together, and I couldn't have been more excited for her. The feedback from her first had been positive, but this time, I was determined to help her truly shine.

The Interview Prep Call

With less than 24 hours to prepare, we jumped straight into action. I wanted Shikha to feel calm, confident, and ready to show up as her best self. To give her that support, I booked a video call with her three hours before the interview to go through everything together.

As I mentioned earlier, we usually schedule our prep calls a few hours beforehand or the day before if the interview is first thing in the morning. That timing gives candidates space to ask last-minute questions, revisit their notes, and properly digest any new information we share with them.

Our prep calls are fairly detailed—we don't just go over the job description. We take the time to get to know our clients beyond the paper brief. This helps us highlight the things that might genuinely appeal to a candidate, and it allows us to spot synergies that might not be obvious at first glance.

We also usually visit our clients onsite, which means we can give practical tips like where to park, how to access the building, or what the general vibe of the office is. These small but thoughtful details help us prepare our candidates holistically—so they're not only ready to answer questions but also to walk in feeling confident, calm, and comfortable in the environment.

At exactly 12 pm on Wednesday, I joined the call with a big, beaming smile, which Shikha returned with her sweet but slightly bemused expression—likely wondering why I was so excited about something as nerve-wracking as an interview.

"I am SO excited for you, Shikha! How are you feeling?" I asked, practically bouncing in my chair.

"Ah, a bit nervous, but I think I'll be fine," she said with a laugh – used to my energy when prepping, giving feedback or celebrating little wins.

Without skipping a beat, I jumped into prep mode with a big smile "Okay, what information did the recruiter give you? How detailed is the position description? What are the working hours? Who's interviewing you? What team will you be joining? How experienced is the interviewer? What's the dress code like?"

Shikha, fully aware of my excitement-fueled interrogation, smiled and forwarded the email she had received from the recruiter.

I opened it while still on the call, scanning for the information that they had sent her and also looking for similarities to what we would normally send our candidates before they attended an interview with either ourselves or our clients.

Shikha had sent me the original SEEK advertisement, which was written by the same recruiter. It came across as quite lacklustre—though, unfortunately, that's not uncommon. Many ads are written quickly, generically, or by people with little training or experience.

I'm not sure why, but I genuinely expected more in the email. Regardless of whether someone sees themselves as a transactional recruiter or not, recruitment is still a professional service. The recruiter is being paid by the client and should therefore have a vested interest in providing clear, detailed communication.

Here's the email she received (names removed):

> *Subject: Interview Confirmation*
>
> *It is my pleasure to confirm your 1st interview with Company Name for the position of XXX – casual role.*
>
> *Day: Wednesday – tomorrow at 3 PM*
>
> *Address: Site Interview – Please see attached visitor direction details. Please ask for [Client First Name] upon arrival.*
>
> *Meeting With: Client First and Last Name – Team Lead*
>
> *I wish you the best of luck with your discussions. Please do not hesitate to contact me should you have any queries.*
>
> *Thanks*

We talked through what the recruiter hadn't provided—the position description, company profile, even the interviewer's background. The email was basic at best. But instead of being discouraged, I reassured her. Lack of information doesn't have to be a disadvantage. It can allow you to steer the conversation where you want it to go.

She brightened up as we reframed the situation. I asked what she had done to prepare. She told me about her outfit (perfect), how she had sorted the transport route, mapped out where to go, and already written down a few smart questions.

I reminded her to bring:

- A printed résumé

- A notebook with question-and-answer prompts

- A bottle of water

- A copy of the job advertisement/interview details

- And to check traffic updates before she left

After doing a bit of research, I sent her the hiring manager's LinkedIn profile, and we went over questions and answers she should keep at the front of her mind.

Before ending the call, I told her, "I've cleared my day—call me before or after if you need anything. You've got this!"

She left the call with the same beaming smile I had joined with. I came out of my office and told my team to cross their fingers and toes for her.

If you know me, you know how excited I get for candidates going for interviews—especially those I've built genuine connections with. Interviews aren't just formalities; they're opportunities to share your story, your value, and your future potential.

Why Preparation is Key

It's always better to be over prepared than under prepared when it comes to interviews. Thorough preparation boosts your confidence and ensures you leave a lasting impression on potential employers.

If you're fortunate enough to have an experienced recruiter, they should help you prepare with insider insights. But as we saw with Shikha, that's not always guaranteed. Owning your preparation—regardless of who's helping—is essential.

Think through the logistics: plan your route, check traffic, and factor in potential delays. Being early is being on time. Being on time is late.

Don't just skim the job advertisement —dig deeper. Understand the department, who the role reports to, and how it connects with broader company goals. This allows you to tailor your answers and ask sharp, relevant questions

Strong interviews don't start with a handshake — they start with preparation. The more you plan ahead, the more confident and in control you'll feel on the day.

Interview prep isn't just about rehearsing answers—it's about doing your homework on the company, the role, and the people involved. Know who you're meeting, what the job actually involves, and how your experience can add value.

Dress in a way that matches the culture of the workplace, and bring everything you need with you — printed documents, a list of thoughtful questions, and a calm, grounded mindset. Even your travel plan can play a role in keeping your nerves down.

Each small action builds your confidence. Preparation builds confidence and gives you control in interviews. It allows you to walk in knowing your value, your story, and the role you're applying for. Even if you don't have all the information, you can still navigate the conversation with clarity and direction.

Shikha's story is a powerful example of what persistence and preparation can achieve. Despite limited feedback and unclear guidance, she leaned into every opportunity and stayed proactive. Her experience reminds us that even in a disorganised system, you can rise by staying consistent, coachable, and committed. Her experience proves that even in a messy or inconsistent process, you can still shine by staying consistent, coachable, and committed.

Use the Interview Preparation Checklist in **Resources and Tools for Success** as your guide. Each step—from researching the company to planning your travel—adds a layer of confidence. Remember, interviews aren't just about responding to questions; they're a chance to steer the conversation and show how you align with the role. Your preparation lets you take that control and leave a lasting impression.

As you continue building on your preparation, the next chapter focuses on one of the most overlooked—yet essential—elements of interview success: understanding the company. It's not enough to simply show up prepared to talk about yourself. You need to demonstrate that you've done your homework and that you're genuinely interested in the organisation and its future.

Let's look at how to gather meaningful insights about your prospective employer and use them to create authentic, informed conversations that go beyond surface-level questions.

Chapter Four
Understanding the Company
How to research, read between the lines, and connect with your future employer

Before your interview, conducting thorough research into the company's background is one of the most crucial steps in your preparation. It's not about memorising a tagline or reciting facts from the 'About Us' page—it's about building a well-rounded understanding of who they are, what they value, and how they operate. Research isn't just about ticking a box; it's about arming yourself with the insight to speak with relevance, connect with purpose, and demonstrate that you've done the work before you've even walked through the door.

A candidate who has taken the time to explore the company's recent projects, market positioning, leadership team, and even tone of voice on social media will always stand out. When you reference a campaign they've run, a value that resonates with you, or an initiative you genuinely admire, it shows more than preparation—it shows curiosity, care, and intention. You're not just applying for *a* job—you're showing up as someone who wants to be part of *their* team. That kind of effort makes conversations richer, more aligned, and ultimately more memorable.

Key Points:
- Strategic research sets you apart from other candidates

- Cultural alignment matters just as much as technical skills

- Solopreneur-led businesses require a different research approach

- Market awareness helps you tailor your value and stand out

Knowing more than just the basics allows you to walk into the room with clarity and confidence, ready to engage in a conversation that feels thoughtful and considered—not transactional. It signals initiative, shows that you've gone the extra mile, and reflects a genuine interest in whether the opportunity is truly the right fit—for both you and the employer.

In a sea of generic applications, candidates who speak with insight and relevance always cut through. Having done your research means your answers won't sound rehearsed—they'll feel authentic. You'll be able to reference a recent announcement, reflect a company value in your own words, or mention a client initiative that genuinely impressed you. These small but powerful details show you've taken the time to connect the dots—and that's exactly the kind of approach most employers are looking for.

While every interview varies, more often than not, there will be a point where the interviewer prompts you to demonstrate how much research you've done. Being prepared for that moment isn't just beneficial—it's expected.

> A question that will often come up is,
> "What do you know about our company?"
> or
> "Why do you want to work here?"

Researching a company can feel overwhelming—especially when there's so much information floating around online. The key is to break it down into manageable steps. Start with the basics: explore the company's website and read through their 'About' page, recent blog posts, and media releases. Then expand your view by checking recent news articles and industry mentions.

As you form a broader view of the company, checking employee reviews and their social media presence can offer deeper insights—a topic we'll explore more fully later in this chapter.

This multi-channel approach helps you form a well-rounded picture of the company's culture, values, and how they're perceived in the market—not just how they present themselves.

And here's a tip I always share: ask your recruiter a few specific questions about the company. Their responses (or lack thereof) can be very telling. An experienced recruiter will know their client well and should be able to talk confidently about the company culture, team dynamics, and expectations for the role. If they're vague, unprepared, or only giving you surface-level details, it might be a red flag—either that they haven't taken the time to build a relationship with the employer, or that you may need to dig deeper before committing to the interview. Either way, it's better to go in with eyes wide open.

The Importance of a Comprehensive Approach

One key area to focus on is the company's history and key milestones. By understanding how the business has evolved and what they're most proud of, you gain insight into their values and direction. Look for turning points—product launches, awards, expansions—that help you understand their story.

Research the leadership team as well. Platforms like LinkedIn are goldmines for seeing the background of CEOs, managers, and team leads. A leader with a background in innovation, for instance, might indicate a dynamic workplace; one with a long tenure in operations may suggest a focus on stability and process.

Stay across any recent news or media coverage. Whether it's a new partnership, rebrand, or merger, referencing these in your interview shows initiative and genuine interest. If you're interviewing with a corporate or ASX-listed company, you may also find their annual report online. It's a useful resource to understand strategy, priorities, and financial health—especially if you're applying for roles in finance, sales, or leadership.

Also consider looking at the company's organisational chart (if available) or team pages on the website. This can help you understand reporting structures, identify potential colleagues, and see how the team is structured. It's particularly useful for assessing where your role fits into the bigger picture and spotting potential career development pathways within the organisation.

Don't overlook the tone of the company's communication either—how they write job ads, newsletters, or social media posts often reflect their values and internal culture. Are they formal and polished, or casual and playful? This can guide how you present yourself in the interview.

Researching a Company Led by a Solopreneur

The influx of entrepreneurs into the business world over the past few years has been, at times, excessive. With this surge has come rapid growth in companies led by excited but often inexperienced founders or solopreneurs who haven't considered how critical the recruitment process is to their long-term success.

In my experience, these businesses usually begin with a brilliant concept. The masterminds behind them get swept up in the momentum, hire reactively, and are typically unprepared when it comes to not only interviews—but also managing their people once they're on board. Finding reliable information about these types of businesses can be tricky.

My advice? Don't get distracted by the glossy website or curated Instagram feed. Look deeper. When interviewing with a small business or solopreneur-led company, your research process might look a little different — but it's just as important. These businesses often reflect the personality and values of their founder, so learning about the individual behind the brand can give you critical insights. Explore their website (especially the About section), check their social media for tone and consistency, and see how they interact with clients or followers. Listen to any podcasts they've appeared on or client interviews they've been tagged in, and pay attention to testimonials or reviews on platforms like Google or LinkedIn.

You'll want to understand how they present themselves, whether they communicate clearly, and if they maintain professional boundaries.

Be mindful of red flags like vague job expectations, inconsistent communication, or a lack of structure.

Working with a solopreneur can be rewarding—but be mindful. Ask questions, trust your gut, and look for signs that their business has a foundation, not just a vision.

Leveraging Social Media and Employee Reviews

Platforms like Facebook, LinkedIn, and Instagram are excellent tools for gauging a company's personality. Look at what they post. Are they showcasing staff milestones? Highlighting community impact? Bragging about long hours? (Red flag.)

Employee reviews on Glassdoor, SEEK, or Google can also offer valuable insight. Don't judge a company on one review—but if you see patterns, pay attention. Praise for leadership, training, or flexibility are good signs. Repeated concerns about turnover or unclear expectations? Worth noting.

If you have mutual connections on LinkedIn, reach out. A five-minute call can give you the kind of real talk a website never will. You can also research the interviewers themselves—find common ground or talking points to help build rapport.

Also, be aware of how companies interact online.

Do they respond to customer comments with professionalism? Are they engaged in their community or industry? Do they affiliate with certain organisations or lean heavily towards a certain tone online?

Public interactions can be a good indicator of internal culture and how they treat people generally.

> "Hire someone that doesn't fit your culture but can positively contribute to it."

Beyond Culture Fit: Hiring for Enrichment

Understanding a company's mission and values isn't just a line on your checklist—it's a way to align with their purpose and culture. These principles often guide internal decision-making and team dynamics. When you can align your own values with theirs, you're not just pitching yourself as a candidate, you're presenting yourself as someone who belongs there. When evaluating a company, it's important not just to ask, "Do I fit in here?"—but also, "Can I add value here?" This is a shift from cultural fit to cultural enrichment.

For hiring to be truly effective, clients must adopt the right attitude towards recruitment. While they have an immediate need to fill a position, they must recognise that the candidate in front of them is likely nervous, full of questions, and genuinely evaluating the opportunity. This mindset is crucial to the success of any recruitment process. As part of my vetting process, I work only with clients who exhibit a strong understanding of the role they're hiring for and the importance of its impact within their organisation.

Clients must acknowledge the value of the hiring process well before crafting the job brief. They need to approach it with humility, understanding that not everyone will leap at the chance to work for them. This respect extends not just to the candidate but to the role itself and its place within the company's vision. As a business owner, I understand that hiring is both a time and financial investment. My role involves ensuring that clients take the process seriously and commit to creating a positive interview experience. This means contributing time, effort, and resources to provide a supportive and engaging environment for candidates.

When clients embrace this mindset, I can confidently assure candidates that they are walking into an organisation that values them as individuals, understands the role they are interviewing for, and has the infrastructure and plans to support new employees. This includes having a clear onboarding strategy and a culture that fosters growth and inclusivity.

Case Study: Why Good Clients Matter

Last year, I was introduced to Meg, the owner of *Third Space Accountants* in Brisbane, through a mutual connection. From our very first meeting, I knew this would be a great partnership. Meg was sharp, open, and genuinely committed to building a team—not just filling seats.

What stood out most about Meg was her approach. She wasn't interested in just hiring someone to do a job. She wanted to bring people in who could grow, thrive, and contribute to the future of the firm. She didn't get caught up in corporate fluff or rigid requirements. Instead, she focused on potential, fit, and long-term value.

Together, we reworked her recruitment and onboarding processes to make them more structured, intentional, and human. We created a framework that allowed for clear expectations, career progression, and a smoother start for new hires. Meg was hands-on but never overbearing—she trusted the process and gave thoughtful input along the way.

One of the things I admire most is how Meg sees the whole person behind a résumé. Whether it was someone on a temporary visa, a returning parent, or a candidate from an unconventional background, she leaned into the conversation. She didn't just "give people a go"—she made space for them to succeed.

Over the past twenty years, I've recruited across all levels for firms, particularly in professional services like legal and accounting. These industries tend to have a very particular way of recruiting. There's often a rigid checklist: a bachelor's degree, a CA or CPA qualification, and a specific "type" of person that fits the culture. Beyond that, there's rarely much flexibility. Salaries are usually at or just above minimum wage for junior or support roles, and there's often little room to move on that. But Meg challenged that mindset. She understood the value of paying people properly and building a culture that attracts talent, not just filters it. She looked past the résumé to the human—and that's what makes her exceptional.

Today, the team at Third Space Accountants is strong, diverse, and genuinely aligned and I still work with Meg and the team not just around recruitment but also career growth for the team. It's a reflection of leadership that prioritises people, communication, and clarity.

Working with clients like Meg reminds me why I do this work. When you partner with someone who respects the process, values their people, and leads with purpose, recruitment becomes a powerful tool for transformation.

What makes a good employer?

The best employers don't just look for someone who blends into their existing environment. They seek individuals who bring new diverse perspectives, fresh ideas, and complementary strengths that enhance team performance and adaptability.

If you're preparing for an interview, this is a powerful mindset shift. You're not there to simply conform. You're there to show how your background, experience, and personality can positively influence and expand the existing culture.

For companies, this particular approach requires openness—welcoming people from different industries, backgrounds, and ways of thinking. For candidates, it means understanding your unique value and having the confidence to articulate it. If a company isn't receptive to that kind of enrichment, it may not be the place where you'll truly grow and it's important that every role you go into is a role that will positively contribute to your career journey.

When you research an organisation, really research and look beyond surface-level culture statements. Instead, try to assess how inclusive and forward-thinking they are in practice.

Ask yourself:

- Do they actively support innovation? Look for evidence of new projects, creative problem-solving, or a willingness to experiment.

- Do they promote from within? This suggests they invest in development and value long-term contribution.

- Is their leadership team diverse? Diversity in leadership often reflects a broader commitment to inclusion and different perspectives.

- Do they have employee resource groups or inclusion initiatives? These can signal a strong internal culture that celebrates difference and supports belonging.

These are all signs of a company that hires for enrichment—not just fit.

One key element I emphasise with clients is the importance of hiring for cultural enrichment rather than mere cultural fit. A great hire doesn't just blend seamlessly into the existing environment but adds value to it, enhancing diversity and driving innovation. This involves seeking candidates from a variety of industries, backgrounds, and experiences. Diversity is not just a box to tick; it's a cornerstone of adaptability and long-term success.

Some clients resist change due to familiarity, past negative experiences, or fears of exposing their own inadequacies. Part of my role is to address these concerns and guide them toward a future-focused approach to hiring. When clients embrace reciprocal growth and the benefits of diversity, they open doors to transformative possibilities within their teams.

This is where insight from an experienced recruiter can be incredibly valuable. My role isn't just about matching résumés to roles—it's about equipping candidates with insider knowledge that goes beyond the job description.

When I speak with clients, I explore what makes their business tick—the story behind their brand, what drives them, and what kind of environment they're trying to create. These conversations help me understand who would thrive in their space and how open they are to new perspectives and personalities.

Understanding not just what a company does, but why they do it—and even who they are beyond work—can make a huge difference. If you find a link between your interests and theirs, that's where the magic happens.

Candidate Case Study: More Than Skills: How Shared Passions Sealed the Deal

I once prepped a candidate for an interview with an engineering firm. During my conversation with the owner, I learned that their love for cars and nostalgic memories of growing up fixing cars with their dad had inspired them to start the business. The candidate, coincidentally, shared that racing cars with their brother was a beloved hobby. Even more impressively, beyond my own insights, the candidate had taken the time to research the company and discovered that it sponsored several racing cars, which aligned perfectly with their personal interests.

This connection became a focal point during the interview. Instead of sticking solely to structured, role-specific questions, the conversation flowed naturally as they discussed their shared interest. The interview took on a more relaxed, authentic tone, helping the candidate build strong rapport and stand out as someone genuinely interested in the company's work and vision.

After being successful in securing the role, the candidate applied not just his skills and experience but his own style of working and aligned it with the company's values and goals. Within six months, he was promoted to a management position and now leads his own team. His ability to align with not just the owner and their story but also the company's culture—while also contributing to it—helped him thrive.

Sometimes the best connections aren't found in your résumé —they're found in your passions.

Understanding the Competitive Landscape

Knowing where a company stands in the market—and who their competitors are—shows that you've thought beyond the role. It positions you as someone who's strategic and commercially aware—traits that are highly valued in any role, but especially in fast-moving, competitive industries.

If you're applying for a marketing or sales position, dig deeper into the company's brand voice, marketing strategy, and audience reach. Explore how they differentiate themselves from competitors—are they innovative, value-driven, niche-focused, or price leaders? Compare their social media engagement, advertising tone, and website messaging with at least two similar businesses. This can help you identify opportunities for improvement, or areas where you could offer value.

In operations, logistics, or product development roles , look at their recent projects, service offerings, delivery model, or customer feedback. What are customers saying in public reviews or forums? Are they leaders in service, innovation, or price—or are they falling behind?

Pay close attention to job ads posted by their competitors for similar roles. What titles are they using? What are the salary ranges? Are there skill requirements or responsibilities that differ? This can give you leverage in understanding your market value, asking informed questions in the interview, or even negotiating salary.

You don't need to present a competitor analysis in your interview, but being able to mention, "I noticed that X and Y companies are investing in [insert trend or product], and I thought it was interesting that your brand has positioned itself differently – what was the motivator behind this approach?," shows you've done your homework and that you understand the broader market context.

This type of insight not only helps you feel more prepared but also shows the employer you're invested in their business—not just your own success. It gives you context—even if the company you're interviewing with is small or niche.

Case Study: No Gov Experience, No Problem

I recently worked with a mentee who was applying for a role within a Federal Government department. While she had solid work experience in the private sector, this was her first time navigating a government recruitment process—which is a completely different ball game. Government roles often come with layers of complexity: selection criteria, formal interview panels, and a strong emphasis on alignment with departmental values and public service principles.

One of the first things we tackled was how to shift her thinking. Rather than trying to research the entire department—which can be overwhelming—I encouraged her to focus on the specific business unit or project the role sat within. This allowed her to tailor her preparation more effectively and understand where her private sector experience could provide real value.

We also walked through how the department fit within the broader government portfolio, what services it delivered, and who the primary stakeholders were. By concentrating on these areas, she was able to reframe her previous experience to highlight transferable skills—like stakeholder communication, time management, and project delivery—while clearly articulating how those aligned with the department's goals and priorities.

To go a step further, she took the initiative to research the interviewers on LinkedIn. That extra effort gave her insight into their professional backgrounds and opened up opportunities to build rapport in the interview. She wasn't just answering questions—she was connecting with the panel and showing that she understood both the role and the environment she was stepping into.

Despite not having any prior government experience, she was successful in securing the role. What made the difference was her commitment to preparation and her ability to translate her existing strengths into the language of public service—showing the panel that she didn't just want the job, she was ready to contribute meaningfully from day one.

Company Research: Know Before You Go

Before any interview, investing time into researching the company is one of the most important steps you can take. It shows initiative, respect for the opportunity, and a genuine interest in the organisation. More importantly, it equips you to speak with clarity and confidence about why you're a great fit — and to assess whether the company is a good fit for you.

Start by understanding the company's mission, values, and services. Read their 'About Us' section and familiarise yourself with any key milestones or defining moments in their history. Explore who's behind the business — review the leadership team's backgrounds on LinkedIn and note their experience, expertise, and professional tone.

Look into any recent news, media coverage, or blog updates to stay up to date with what they've been working on. This can include new partnerships, product launches, or internal growth. It's also worth checking their presence on platforms like LinkedIn, Instagram, or Facebook. Observe how they communicate online — the tone, content, and level of engagement can offer insight into how they operate internally.

Review employee feedback on sites like Glassdoor, SEEK, or Google reviews to get a feel for the company's culture, leadership style, and internal communication. Research who their clients are, what industries they serve, and how they position themselves in the market compared to their competitors.

Dig into any current projects or initiatives that reflect their strategic direction or innovation, and take time to understand the company's organisational structure — especially where your potential role fits and who you might be working with.

Lastly, look up your interviewer's profile. Understanding their background can help you find common ground and ask more tailored questions during the interview. And perhaps most importantly, reflect on whether this is a place where you can see yourself growing. Do their values align with yours? Would you feel proud to represent their brand?

For a full, detailed checklist to guide your research — covering everything from company culture to competitive landscape — refer to the Company Research Checklist in **Resources and Tools for Success.**

Thoroughly understanding the company you're interviewing with is more than just a preparatory step—it's a way to empower yourself. It gives you the confidence to answer questions with context, ask thoughtful questions that demonstrate your engagement, and ultimately position yourself as someone who's not just looking for a job, but someone who genuinely wants to contribute to the company's success. When you've done your research, you'll feel more prepared, more capable, and more in control of the conversation.

As you delve into researching the company, remember to balance your findings with self-reflection. Consider how your skills, values, and experiences align with what you've learned about the organisation. This isn't just about impressing your interviewer—it's also about determining if this is the right environment for you. A well-prepared candidate doesn't just sell themselves; they also make an informed decision about whether the company is the right fit for their goals.

In the next chapter, *Overcoming Interview Anxiety*, we'll explore practical techniques to help you stay composed and focused when it matters most. From managing pre-interview nerves to reframing self-doubt, this chapter will walk you through some of the most common—and often overlooked—barriers to interview success.

Whether you've ever found yourself blanking out mid-answer, over-explaining to fill silences, or leaving the room second-guessing everything you said, you're not alone. Anxiety shows up in many forms, and it can derail even the most prepared candidate. The good news? It's absolutely manageable.

Ace Your Interview isn't just about mastering tactics and frameworks; it's about building the mindset that allows you to walk into any room and own your story with confidence and clarity. So, if nerves have ever gotten the better of you—or you're simply ready to feel more in control—turn the page.

We're about to dive into one of the most universally challenging aspects of the interview process and transform it into one of your biggest strengths.

Chapter Five
Overcoming Interview Anxiety
Reframing Nerves as a Pathway to Confidence

Feeling nervous before an interview is natural — and it doesn't matter if you're applying for your first role or your twenty-first.

The fear of the unknown often dominates in the lead-up to an interview, whether it's with me, the recruiter, the client, or in subsequent rounds. Anxiety stems from the stakes involved, the pressure to perform, and the uncertainty about what lies ahead.

Yet, it's important to remember that interviews are not interrogations — they are conversations. Opportunities to share your story, your value, and your potential.

Key Points:

- Anxiety is Normal – It's a natural response, not a weakness.

- It's a Conversation – Think of interviews as two-way chats.

- Preparation Calms Nerves – The more you prepare, the more confident you feel.

- Lean on Your Support – Encouragement from others can boost your mindset.

At its core, overcoming interview anxiety begins with preparation and mindset. This principle underpins how I approach my work, not just with candidates but also with clients.

For candidates, the focus is on building confidence, addressing uncertainties, and presenting their authentic selves.

For clients, it's about fostering a recruitment process that values the person behind the application, ensuring a respectful and supportive environment for interviews.

Creating this balance helps reduce the anxiety that candidates feel while also giving clients the best chance to connect with talent on a human level.

One of the most effective ways to calm your nerves before an interview is to reach out to someone in your network who believes in you. Whether it's a friend, family member, or mentor, these people can provide that much-needed boost.

Strong networks are invaluable — not just in your career, but in every aspect of life. They consist of the people who support you, uplift you, and help you stay grounded and accountable.

Preparation isn't only about knowing how to answer tough questions — it's about helping someone feel genuinely ready to walk into a room and own their story.

Often, what holds candidates back isn't a lack of skill — it's anxiety, imposter syndrome, or simply not knowing how to frame their experience in a way that resonates.

I see it as my responsibility to help strip some of that fear away and replace it with clarity and confidence.

For instance, at the tail end of my conversation with Shikha, even though her confidence had visibly grown during our call, I felt it was important to reiterate my belief in her abilities — instilling a deeper sense of self-assurance and calm before she stepped into the unknown.

Shikha's Story Continued

"You've absolutely got this, Shikha," I told her with complete sincerity during our prep call. "You've got the skills, the experience, and the presence. You communicate beautifully in person, and you'll be a genuine asset to this company."

I meant every word. I was so excited for her—this was exactly what we'd been working toward, and I wanted her to feel supported all the way through. I reminded her that the person interviewing her had once been in her shoes. They had to interview for their role too, and they'd likely appreciate the effort she was putting in.

"He's got a strong technical background, just like you," I added. "That's important—but so are your soft skills. The way you interact, adapt, and respond under pressure matters just as much."

All of this was genuine—she interviewed and communicated wonderfully. My advice came not only from having worked with her closely but also from coaching and preparing thousands of candidates before her.

Giving her the security of knowing that I was there if she needed me, and normalising the human side of the interviewer, were vital parts of our conversation. Reinforcing her experience as not just transferable but deeply relevant to the role was the final piece of encouragement she needed.

These small but significant reminders can make all the difference when someone is about to take a big step forward in their career.

> "Does your story stack up? Here's the truth: It does. And it's often the very thing that makes you stand out"

Reframing Your Unique Background as a Strength

One of the biggest sources of interview anxiety is the internal voice that says, "I don't quite fit the mould." Maybe your degree isn't directly related. Maybe you've worked in a different industry. Maybe you've taken time out to raise a family, explore a different path, or move countries.

Different doesn't mean lesser. It means you bring a unique lens—something the company may not even know it needs yet. Whether you've worked in hospitality, retail, construction, education, or a completely unrelated sector, those experiences are packed with transferable skills. Communication, time management, leadership under pressure, working with diverse people—these aren't just "add-ons," they are core competencies that often separate high performers from average ones.

But here's the catch: you have to own it first.

When I work with candidates, one of the most powerful shifts we make is reframing. Instead of saying, "I don't have direct experience," we start asking:

- What has my past taught me that applies here?

- How did I solve problems in my last role?

- What makes my approach or insight different—and valuable?

For example, someone transitioning from hospitality into a lab role might feel out of place at first. But when they start to realise that managing a kitchen during a lunch rush demands fast decision-making, attention to detail, whilst juggling different tasks and handling pressure while communicating clearly - suddenly, that experience holds weight. It means something.

This shift is crucial. It turns anxiety into empowerment and that's where I want you to be when you feel like your experience, story or background may not be relevant or important.

You're no longer walking into the interview hoping they won't notice what you lack. You're walking in ready to highlight what you bring. When you speak about your background with confidence and clarity, you give the interviewer permission to see it as an asset, too.

And if you feel yourself spiralling into doubt, remind yourself of this: no one else has your exact journey. No one else has seen what you've seen, overcome what you've overcome, or grown through the same circumstances. That makes your perspective valuable—if you're brave enough to show it.

So instead of trying to fit in, focus on standing out—for all the right reasons.

Drawing Parallels Between Clients and Candidates

Interestingly, many of the fears and concerns candidates have mirror those of clients. Both parties worry about making the right impression, whether they'll be liked, or if their efforts will lead to the desired outcome. Recognising these parallels creates an opportunity for empathy and mutual respect during the interview process. By understanding that both sides are navigating their own anxieties and aspirations, candidates can approach interviews with a sense of shared humanity rather than intimidation.

Understanding clients' challenges and expectations allows me to prepare candidates more effectively. By humanising the clients and helping candidates see them as relatable individuals with their own apprehensions and goals, I create a bridge of empathy between the two parties. This shared understanding often alleviates some of the candidate's anxiety, making the interview process less intimidating.

For candidates, anxiety often stems from the fear of the unknown and potential missteps. Common worries include making mistakes, forgetting prepared answers, misinterpreting questions, arriving late, or saying the wrong thing. These concerns can feel overwhelming, but with the right preparation, they can be managed effectively.

One of the first steps in tackling interview anxiety is normalising it. Every candidate should know that it's okay to feel nervous. The goal isn't to eliminate anxiety entirely but to channel it constructively. Preparation is the most effective tool in this regard. This involves researching the company, rehearsing answers to potential questions, and practising non-verbal communication such as maintaining eye contact and using confident body language.

Equally important is addressing the mindset. Candidates often place unnecessary pressure on themselves to deliver perfection. I encourage them to focus on authenticity instead. Employers aren't looking for robotic perfection; they want to see the real person and understand how their skills, personality, and values align with the company's goals.

Ultimately, overcoming interview anxiety is about building confidence through preparation, mindset, and connection. For candidates, this means feeling prepared and supported. For clients, it involves creating an environment that values candidates as individuals and partners in their company's growth. When both parties approach the process with mutual respect and a shared goal of finding the right match, interviews become less about judgment and more about discovery.

Managing Anxiety with Preparation and Relaxation Techniques

One of the most effective ways to manage pre-interview anxiety is to combine solid preparation with simple relaxation techniques. It's completely normal to feel nervous—interviews can feel high-stakes, especially when you really want the job. But with the right tools, you can turn that nervous energy into something useful. Rather than trying to eliminate anxiety altogether (which often isn't realistic), aim to acknowledge it and channel it into calm, focused momentum.

Practices such as deep breathing can help you feel more grounded and in control. For example, deep breathing exercises are a quick and accessible way to soothe your nervous system. Before an interview, take a moment to sit quietly, inhale deeply for four counts, hold for four counts, and exhale slowly for another four counts. Repeat this cycle a few times to help reduce tension and bring your attention back to the present.

Visualisation is another powerful strategy. Picture yourself walking confidently into the interview room, speaking with clarity, and connecting well with your interviewer. Imagine leaving the space feeling proud of how you showed up. This mental rehearsal not only helps settle your nerves but also primes your mind to follow through with the confidence you've already visualised. These simple but powerful techniques can make a significant difference in how you feel—and how you perform—on the day.

Mock interviews are another invaluable way to prepare. Whether you're practising with a friend, mentor, or career coach, these sessions allow you to simulate the interview environment in a low-pressure setting. They give you the opportunity to refine your responses, experiment with different ways of framing your experience, and receive honest, constructive feedback. Over time, this process not only builds your confidence but also helps you become more comfortable with the format and flow of interviews. The more familiar the experience feels, the less intimidating the real thing becomes.

The key is to build small habits into your preparation that support both your mind and your message. A well-prepared candidate with a calm, focused mindset will always stand out—because it's not just what you say, but how you carry yourself that leaves a lasting impression. Interview anxiety doesn't have to hold you back. With the right techniques, it can become part of your process—not a barrier to your success.

ACE YOUR INTERVIEW

The Power of Body Language: The "Superhero Pose"

Another simple yet powerful technique to help boost your confidence before an interview is the "superhero pose," popularised by social psychologist Amy Cuddy in her 2012 TED Talk Your Body Language Shapes Who You Are. Cuddy's research, published in Psychological Science, explores how expansive, open postures—like standing tall with your hands on your hips, chest lifted, and head held high—can increase feelings of confidence and reduce stress. These poses aren't just about looking powerful; they can actually shift your internal state, helping your brain register strength and calm before a high-pressure situation like an interview.

Years ago, before I was running workshops, hosting podcasts, or confidently speaking at events and on panels, I came across the idea of the power pose. I remember laughing the first time I tried it—mostly because the image of me standing like Wonder Woman in my bedroom was a bit ridiculous. I imagined someone walking in and seeing me mid-pose, hands on hips, chin up, chest out, channelling superhero energy with zero context. But here's the thing—it worked. Maybe it was the placebo effect, or maybe it was the laughter that loosened me up, but it gave me a noticeable boost. It broke the tension, shifted my focus, and made me feel just a little more in control.

Since then, I've shared this technique with people from all walks of life—regardless of age, gender, or cultural background—and the reaction is almost always the same. First, they laugh – actually I laugh too whilst explaining it. But then they try it – and more often than not, they come back to me and say, "It actually helped." I even set it as homework sometimes.

It's not about pretending to be someone you're not—it's about reminding yourself that you already have everything you need within you. The pose forces you to physically take up space, and with that comes a subtle mental shift. You stand a little taller, you feel a little braver, and you go into the interview with a bit more certainty than you had before. I still do it—less often these days, but when I need that extra lift, it's always in my back pocket. Recently someone told me, "If it works for you and gives you that boost, I'll try anything to get over my nerves," and I smiled—because that's exactly what it does.

So, before stepping into your next interview, find a private space—even a restroom cubicle or a quiet corner—and strike your superhero pose. Hold it for one to two minutes. You might feel a bit awkward or silly but that's okay. That brief moment of silliness could be exactly what you need to feel grounded, energised, and ready. This small physical shift can have a powerful psychological impact, helping you walk into the room with a sense of calm self-assurance. Sometimes, the smallest rituals have the biggest ripple effect.

Connecting Relaxation Techniques to Your Mindset

These relaxation techniques and the power pose aren't just about calming your nerves—they're about shifting your mindset. When combined with thorough preparation, they can help you approach the interview with a sense of control. By focusing on what you can manage—your breathing, posture, and preparation—you redirect your energy away from self-doubt and into confidence. It's this shift that can transform anxiety into a powerful tool for success.

For candidates like Shikha, these techniques were game-changing. As her confidence grew during our preparation call, I encouraged her to use a combination of these methods. Shikha left that conversation not just with practical advice but also with a renewed belief in herself—a belief that translated into her stellar interview performance.

When you combine these strategies, you give yourself the best chance to succeed—not by eliminating nerves, but by learning how to work with them. Confidence doesn't always mean being completely calm—it means showing up with clarity, composure, and the ability to channel your energy in the right direction.

The Importance of Connection and Community

As much as interviews are about preparation and presence, they're also about people. And one of the most powerful things you can do—before, during, and after an interview—is to connect with the right people.

That might mean reaching out for feedback after a rejection. It might be calling someone you trust the night before an interview just to hear, "You've got this." Or it might mean working with a mentor or coach who sees your potential even when you're questioning it.

You don't have to do this alone. In fact, you shouldn't.

The people in your corner—those who listen, guide, and reflect your strengths back to you—can make all the difference in how you prepare and how you show up. They'll help you reframe doubts, clarify your message, and build the confidence that doesn't always come from within. Sometimes, it's borrowed. And that's okay.

Whether it's a friend, a former colleague, a recruiter, or someone who's walked this path before—you deserve support that's grounded, honest, and encouraging.

Interviews can feel personal, but they're not a test of worth. They're a chance to connect. And the more you surround yourself with people who remind you of that—people who know your value, even when you temporarily forget it—the more empowered you'll be to walk into that room and own your story.

Because in the end, no strategy, mindset, or pose is more powerful than knowing someone truly believes in you. And sometimes, that's all it takes to believe in yourself too.

And that's where non-verbal communication steps in. Because it's not just about what you say in an interview—it's how you say it, how you carry yourself, and how you read the room. The impression you make begins the moment you walk through the door, long before you've even said a word.

Whether it's a firm handshake, eye contact, the way you sit, or how you respond to silence—your non-verbal cues speak volumes. In many ways, your body language is your first language in an interview. It tells the story of your confidence, your professionalism, and your readiness—often before you've had the chance to speak.

So if nerves are the noise, presence is the volume control.

In the next chapter, we'll explore how to master the silent signals—those subtle but powerful tools that help you hold space, connect authentically, and leave a lasting impression. Because sometimes, how you show up speaks louder than what you say.

Chapter Six
The Power of Non-Verbal Communication

Mastering Presence: Reading the Room and Owning the Space

Before you speak, your body already has. From the moment you enter the building, you're on. Every handshake, nod, pause, and gesture is part of your interview—even the ones you think no one notices. This chapter isn't about putting on a show or being robotic or putting on an act. It's about genuine awareness. It's about showing up fully, reading the energy of the room, and matching it in a way that still feels like you.

Key Points:

- Your interview starts the moment you walk in— not when the questions begin.

- Reading the room is a skill that takes presence, not just preparation.

- Non-verbal cues like posture, eye contact, and tone often leave a stronger impression than what you say.

- Mirroring professionalism, managing your energy, and staying consistent across all stages of the process is what sets candidates apart.

A Note from Me

Typically, my process involves a phone screen and sometimes a video interview before meeting candidates face-to-face. For more senior or client-facing roles, I'll often meet candidates at a café or restaurant. Why? Because how you handle yourself in an everyday, slightly unpredictable environment gives me a lot more insight than a polished response ever could.

I'm observing how you greet the staff, how you sit, whether you stay present in the conversation or get distracted by your surroundings.

I once had a candidate who absolutely nailed the video stage. Sharp, articulate, on point. But in person? They turned up in gym gear, didn't shake my hand when they arrived, and barked at the waitress for getting their coffee order wrong. That five-minute exchange told me more about how they'd represent my client than any résumé ever could.

Spoiler alert: they didn't get the job. And when I checked their references? The stories lined up.

Mirroring the Room

Sometimes in interviews, I'll deliberately adopt a more relaxed posture, speak casually, or go slightly off-script. It's not to throw people off—it's to see if they shift with me. Do they stay grounded and professional, or do they start mirroring my slouch and losing their formality altogether? It's a small but powerful way to see how well someone reads the room.

If the person interviewing you seems chilled and informal, that doesn't mean you throw away all your polish. You can let your guard down slightly, of course—but your tone, posture, and focus should still communicate that you're there to do a job. Remember: confidence is about composure, not comfort. You can be likeable and personable without losing your edge.

The Lasting Impression

Every part of the interview process matters. Whether it's a casual coffee meeting, a panel interview, or a quick video call, people are watching—often more closely than you realise. And it's not just the hiring manager. It could be the receptionist, the EA walking past, or even the barista at the café. Their impressions matter too—especially in workplaces where culture and team fit are key.

I've had clients make decisions based on how candidates treated others in the building. One candidate smiled and thanked every person they met—even complimented the receptionist on her organisation. That same receptionist later told the hiring manager how impressed she was. That small gesture reinforced everything the candidate had said in the interview—and guess what? They got the job.

So the golden rule? Stay consistent. Be respectful, be present, and remember that you're always communicating—even when you're not speaking.

The Skill of Awareness

One of the most overlooked, yet powerful, interview skills is something that's not taught in school or found on a checklist: awareness. It's the ability to walk into a space, take in the atmosphere, pick up on subtle cues, and adapt accordingly. Reading the room isn't just about watching the body language of others—it's about tuning into the energy of the interaction and responding in a way that feels natural, intentional, and respectful.

This is the difference between someone who's technically prepared and someone who's truly present. You could have the perfect résumé, all the right talking points, and even the best intentions—but if you're not aware of how you're being received or the context you're stepping into, you risk disconnecting from the people sitting across from you.

I've seen it too many times. A candidate can ace the phone screen—polite, polished, articulate—and then fall apart when they meet the hiring manager face-to-face. I remember one candidate in particular: great credentials, glowing references, confident during our call. Everything suggested they'd be a standout. But when she walked into the client meeting, it was a completely different story. She showed up late without acknowledging it, launched into answers before questions were finished, and gave responses that felt vague and disconnected. The client felt she was dismissive. In reality, she was nervous—but she masked that discomfort by talking too much and failing to pick up on the room's cues. That interview cost her the role. *What was missing in this interview wasn't intelligence or experience—it was awareness.*

Awareness is what allows you to course-correct in real time. It's what helps you slow your speech when you notice someone struggling to keep up, or dial back your intensity when the room feels more reserved. It's pausing before jumping into your answer so the interviewer can finish their thought. It's catching that moment when someone leans in with curiosity—or withdraws with doubt—and adjusting your delivery accordingly.

Being aware doesn't mean being performative. It means staying grounded, noticing what's happening in the space around you, and choosing how to show up in that moment. When you can do that? You don't just leave a good impression—you leave the right one.

Building Interview Awareness

Awareness isn't something you're born with—it's something you learn, develop, and sharpen over time. Like any skill, it takes a mix of experience, observation, and self-reflection. In interviews, awareness means being present enough to notice the signals the interviewer is sending—both verbal and non-verbal—and knowing how to respond without losing your rhythm.

It could be as simple as picking up on an interviewer leaning in with interest—that's your sign to go a little deeper, to build on what you're saying. On the flip side, if they're glancing at the clock, shifting in their seat, or breaking eye contact, it's likely time to wrap up your point or pivot the conversation. These moments don't need to rattle you—they're opportunities to recalibrate. But you'll only notice them if you're paying attention.

I've worked with candidates who were so focused on getting their points across that they completely missed the mood in the room. One in particular had rehearsed her answers to the point that she was reciting them, almost word-for-word, with no pause for interaction. The interviewer couldn't get a word in. He nodded politely, but I could see the disconnection forming. She wasn't rude or unprepared—just unaware. She was in presentation mode, not conversation mode.

This is where pacing comes in. Start the interview by simply observing. Before diving into your story or your strengths, read the room. What's the energy like? Are you walking into a fast-paced, high-energy environment—or something more measured and formal? Let that shape your tone and delivery.

Throughout the conversation, check in with yourself. Are you talking too much? Are you giving the interviewer time to respond, react, or guide the flow? A good interview should feel like a rhythm—not a monologue. The goal isn't to power through your script; it's to have a genuine, engaging exchange.

And don't underestimate the basics. Arriving early, maintaining eye contact, and having a natural, confident posture already sets a strong foundation. It shows respect for the process and signals that you're present, engaged, and taking the opportunity seriously.

The more interviews you do, the more instinctive this becomes. But even early on, you can start to build your awareness by being curious.

Ask yourself: how am I being received right now? What's the vibe in this space? Is it time to expand or time to simplify? That kind of self-awareness—not just about what you say, but how and when you say it—is what separates someone who interviews well from someone who connects.

Non-Verbal Cues Speak Louder Than Words

Non-verbal communication can be the quiet advantage—or the silent red flag—in any interview. While your words matter, how you present yourself shapes the story the interviewer walks away with. From posture and eye contact to the way you carry your voice, your presence can reinforce your message or completely contradict it.

Before you've even spoken, you're already communicating. That first impression is formed in seconds—how you walk into the room, the way you greet people, your body language as you sit—these all contribute to how you're perceived. A confident candidate doesn't just have strong answers; they have presence, intention, and control over how they engage.

Start with the basics. Walk in tall, offer a warm and professional greeting, and if it's in person, a firm handshake goes a long way. If it's virtual, maintain eye level with your camera, and begin with a calm, open energy. Once seated, your posture should show you're engaged—upright but relaxed, leaning slightly forward to signal interest. Avoid crossing your arms or fidgeting with your hands. These habits, while small, can shift the tone of the entire conversation.

Let your face reflect the message you're sharing. Smiling at the right moments, maintaining natural eye contact, and showing a genuine reaction to what's being said all create a connection. It's not about putting on a performance—it's about aligning your body language with your words.

And then there's tone. Even though it's part of your speech, your tone, pace, and rhythm are all non-verbal indicators of confidence and clarity. Speak with intention. If you need a second to think, pause. There's strength in silence—it shows composure and thoughtfulness.

Finally, consider your surroundings. Whether you're in a boardroom or joining remotely, what you bring with you matters. Keep the table clear of clutter. Phones should be away. Have a notebook or your résumé on hand, but stay focused on the interaction, not your materials. If you're offered water, take small sips at natural breaks—never while mid-sentence.

Quick Reminders: Non-Verbal Cues That Matter

- **Eye Contact** – Stay engaged without staring. Steady, natural eye contact shows confidence and attentiveness.

- **Handshake (or Greeting)** – Firm, warm, and authentic. Online? Begin with a clear and intentional hello.

- **Posture** – Sit upright, lean slightly forward, and avoid slouching. Your body should show you're present and interested.

- **First Impressions Count** – From the reception desk to the interview chair, everything you do is part of the interview.

- **Tone of Voice** – Calm, clear, and well-paced. Avoid rushing or trailing off.

- **Facial Expressions** – Be aware of micro expressions—don't let nerves show as frustration or disinterest.

- **Gestures** – Keep them open and natural. Don't overdo it, and avoid fidgeting.

- **Read the Room** – Watch for nods, disengagement, or time signals from the interviewer and adapt as needed.

- **No Distractions** – Phone off. Watch off. Stay focused.

- **Bring What Matters** – A notebook, your résumé, and thoughtful questions—nothing more, nothing unnecessary.

Looking Ahead: The Words That Matter Most

By now, you've probably realised that interviews aren't just about giving the right answers—they're about creating the right impression. It's how you show up, how you hold space in a room, and how your presence reinforces the story you're telling.

But of course, what you say still matters. When we shift into the actual questions being asked in interviews, it's not just about preparing rehearsed answers—it's about understanding why those questions are being asked in the first place. Great candidates know how to speak with intention, but they also know how to align their responses with the needs of the role and the values of the business.

You've now got what you need to tackle the most common interview questions with confidence and authenticity—sharing your story in a way that actually connects. But it doesn't stop there. In the next chapter, we move into the questions that reveal how you operate when it counts—under pressure, in teams, and when challenges arise. This is where your experience becomes evidence, and where preparation gives you the edge.

This next chapter takes you there. It unpacks the behavioural and situational questions you're most likely to face and shows you how to approach them with strategy, clarity, and confidence—without ever sounding scripted. Because when your words match your presence? That's where the magic happens.

Chapter Seven
Mastering Common Interview Questions
Laying the groundwork for confidence, connection, and clarity

In this chapter, we're focusing on the questions you'll almost always be asked—yet many people still stumble over them. These are the ones that open conversations, form first impressions, and test how well you can connect your story to the role in front of you.

Sadly, common interview questions haven't really changed much in the past twenty years. The language may be slightly different, but the intention remains the same. And let's be honest—sometimes the way they're asked can feel robotic, dry, and overly rehearsed, both for the interviewer and the candidate. But here's the thing: that doesn't make them any less important. I call these 'vetting questions' because that's exactly what they do. If you've been to an interview recently, chances are you've heard one—if not all—of them. Your job is to bring life to them.

Let's break down the 'vetting' stage of interviews, help you reframe traditional questions to highlight your strengths, and prepare you to enter any interview with more clarity, intention, and calm.

Key Points:
- Preparation breeds confidence – Common questions might seem straightforward, but preparing your answers allows you to con-

nect your story clearly and authentically.

- Every role is relevant – Don't discount your past experience. Skills are transferable, and the way you talk about them can position you powerfully.

- Reframe to reveal – Whether it's strengths or weaknesses, how you frame your answer shows self-awareness, not perfection.

- Connection over perfection – Interviews aren't about rehearsed scripts. They're about showing who you are and how you work with others.

When interviewing, depending on who you're meeting with, you can expect a series of common interview questions, whether conducted over the phone or in person if no initial call was made. It's crucial to anticipate these questions, especially in second or third interview rounds with different interviewers or when the interviewer isn't the one who scheduled your meeting. Before your interview, it's essential to think about how you'll respond to these questions, and having a notebook or résumé handy can be useful if you need to jog your memory.

A good interview should feel natural, with a flowing conversation and specific, relevant questions tailored to the position. An experienced interviewer should be able to ask these questions in a creative and engaging manner.

Typically, common interview questions are addressed either during a phone screen or in the initial formal interview stage. Some companies may request answers through forms, video responses, or automated processes during the application. However, skipping steps in the interview process reflects poorly on recruiting practices. These questions establish the foundation for interaction between the interviewer and interviewee, aiming to assess initial fit, suitability, and whether the application should move forward.

In recruitment we call common interview questions "vetting" questions. It's the first part of determining whether the candidate meets the initial criteria and whether we need to prompt or delve further or simply determine them unsuitable.

Often, with all interview questions, it's less about the answer and more about how you answer it. An experienced interviewer will look for signs where the potential employee may be fabricating an answer or hasn't put much thought into their interview preparation.

Shikha's Story Continued

During my time mentoring Shikha, we worked extensively on bridging the gap between her past experiences and the technical expertise required for roles in her desired field. This process involved crafting responses to both common and technical interview questions, a challenge that Shikha initially found daunting. Her main hesitation lay in discussing her recent experience in hospitality, which she felt was unrelated to her career aspirations in molecular biology.

Halfway through our interview preparation, Shikha shared a key concern: "I'm comfortable outlining my technical experience and talking about the work I did as a researcher. I just feel nervous answering the common interview questions they ask, and I'm not sure how to deliver my responses without getting too nervous. My only recent experience has been in hospitality, and I don't feel this is relevant to the role at all, given it's not in the field I studied."

> "Here's an important side note, reader: Every role you've worked in is relevant to future roles you're applying for."

"Working in hospitality isn't just about food preparation and serving customers," I explained to Shikha. "It requires performing multiple tasks at once, mentoring junior staff, managing customers' expectations, adhering to safety and compliance protocols, and ensuring reports and documentation are accurately recorded. These are transferable skills. When answering questions, be honest, but make sure to highlight your strengths and discuss areas where you want to improve."

Her initial reaction was one of surprise, but as we delved deeper, she began to see the value in her hospitality experience. "Some of the main interview questions seem a bit generic," she said. "How do I provide more than just a basic answer?"

Crafting the Perfect "Tell Me About Yourself" Response

"Okay," I said, pausing for effect. "I know you well enough to predict your answers, but the block here is how to translate them into an interview response, right?" Shikha nodded again.

"When we first started, you told me what you enjoy outside of work, what you like to do on weekends, and why you started your degree," I reminded her. She started smiling, clearly seeing where I was going. "That's how you answer the 'Tell me about yourself' question," I said.

Shikha laughed. "Okay, so I would say: 'I moved here a few years ago to study my Bachelor's and continued to my Master's. I've enjoyed travelling around parts of Australia and made some great friends along the way. I volunteer in my spare time, love reading, and have a few other interests. I've always wanted to study this field because I discovered it in high school and found it really interesting.'"

"Perfect," I replied with a smile. "Genuine, and it just flowed naturally. You're simply talking about yourself, leading into why you chose this field, and connecting it to the role you applied for. Simple!" Her laughter returned, this time accompanied by a sense of relief.

Addressing Strengths and Weaknesses

"Next, let's talk about strengths and weaknesses," I continued. "You know your answers, but let's go over them. Strengths are about what you're good at, where you've received positive feedback, and what you can do well with minimal supervision. As for weaknesses, I prefer to reframe them as areas for improvement. The word 'weakness' sounds harsh, but focusing on areas where you want to grow shows humility and a willingness to learn."

"Yes," Shikha began thoughtfully, "so my strengths are being organised at work, managing different tasks, and, when I was a research student, making sure I recorded everything accurately. Also, in my current job, I document everything and ensure health and safety standards are met." She hesitated before adding, "But my weakness is that I haven't worked in my field of study for over a year, and I've never worked in this type of role before."

"Strengths—nailed it," I said encouragingly. "This role needs someone open to learning, perhaps at a slower pace than your current role, but also someone organised who can record things accurately for other team members or business units."

I then tackled her concerns about weaknesses. "As for weaknesses—or rather, improvements—here's how to frame it: Even though you haven't worked in your field for a year, you've continued researching and staying updated on industry breakthroughs. You want your next role to provide not just experience in your field but also an opportunity to work within a team that values both your academic background and your willingness to grow. You have the ability to do this role, and you're looking for an environment that will help you hone your skills."

Practice Builds Confidence

Shikha's confidence grew as we rehearsed these responses. We practised different ways of delivering them until they felt natural and authentic. By the end of our session, she was ready to tackle her upcoming interview.

Before we wrapped up, I reminded Shikha of one last thing: "Every interview is an opportunity to showcase your unique skills and experiences. Don't let nerves hold you back. Trust in your preparation, speak from the heart, and remember—you have so much to offer."

This is a reminder to every candidate: preparation is key. It's not about being perfect—it's about being yourself, knowing your strengths, and showing how you can add value. Your experiences, no matter how unrelated they may seem, are part of what makes you unique. Use them to tell your story and stand out.

The Power of Authenticity in Interviews

"In any interview, the interviewer is looking for more than just your answer; it's about how you answer it," I explained. "One-word or one-sentence responses can come across as robotic. Most common questions are easy to predict—'Tell me about yourself,' 'What are your strengths and weaknesses,' 'What's your biggest achievement.' But you can anticipate these and volunteer answers for other questions at the same time."

Pointing to my notebook, I added, "If you have your answers prepared, you can always refer to your notes if you get stuck during the interview. Preparation gives you confidence."

Shikha nodded, her expression more thoughtful now. "I've got the answers we've gone through, but my main worry, aside from talking about my current experience, is telling them about myself, discussing my strengths and weaknesses, and showing that I'm a reliable worker who can handle multiple tasks."

Tell Me About Yourself

Interestingly, a lot of people find this question unexpectedly challenging to answer, despite it being one of the most frequently asked by hiring managers. While it may seem simple on the surface, this question is designed to help interviewers gauge cultural fit, alignment with the manager or team, and an initial impression of your personality and priorities.

When preparing candidates for interviews, I usually focus on helping them understand what the company is looking for and, if possible, a bit about the interviewer's personality or style. These insights can make a significant difference in how candidates frame their responses. It's not just about reciting your résumé —it's about weaving a narrative that connects who you are with the role and the company's culture.

> During interviews, I often ask candidates to do an exercise: think of three words their coworkers would use to describe them if we called for a reference and three words their friends might use to describe them

It's a great way to start thinking about the qualities that define you both professionally and personally. For example, co-workers might say you're diligent, efficient, and detail-oriented, while friends might say you're funny, caring, and adventurous.

Together, these insights help you build a more holistic picture of yourself to present in the interview.

This question also gives you the opportunity to touch on personal interests or hobbies if you're comfortable doing so. It's an invitation to share what drives you, what you value, and how you approach your work—which often gives the interviewer better insight than your résumé ever could.

If you're ever unsure how much detail to go into, don't be afraid to ask, "What would you like to know?" It's a great way to steer the conversation in a direction that benefits you and helps keep your answer focused on what matters most to the interviewer.

Talking About Strengths and Weaknesses

This is one of the most common interview questions—and also one of the most misunderstood. It's not designed to trip you up. It's there to see if you actually *know* yourself, and whether you've taken time to reflect on how you work, what you bring, and what you're still working on. Interviewers aren't looking for perfection. They're looking for insight.

I often say to candidates: "This is your chance to own what makes you valuable." But it's not about saying you're a *workhorse* or that you just *get in and get it done*. That's not a strength—that's burnout waiting to happen. Instead, think about your strengths as a combination of what comes naturally to you, where you've received positive feedback, and what you enjoy doing. Bonus points if you can back it up with results or examples.

Try these prompts to reflect on your strengths:

- What do you do well with little or no guidance?

- What type of work do others come to you for?

- What do you enjoy or find easy?

- When was the last time you got positive feedback—and what was it for?

When it comes to weaknesses, I always tell candidates to imagine my voice in their head asking: *"What's something you want to improve on?"* Because that's what this question is really about. Don't list personal flaws or self-deprecate. This isn't the place for "I care too much" or "I work too hard." It's about showing that you're aware of your development areas, and more importantly, that you're doing something about them.

Here's how to reframe your thinking around weaknesses:

- What's something you've had to consciously work on?

- What's a skill or trait you know you need to build on for your next role?

- Is there a part of the job you'd love more exposure or mentorship in?

And remember: owning a weakness doesn't make you look bad. Pretending you don't have one does. What interviewers want to hear is how you've identified the gap, what you've done about it, and how it won't stop you from being successful in the role.

Put simply:

- Strengths are your *value-add*. Speak with clarity and confidence.

- Weaknesses are your *growth edges*. Show honesty, humility, and initiative.

It's not about perfection—it's about self-awareness, direction, and progress. And if you can deliver that with confidence and real-world examples, you'll stand out. By preparing a few clear, authentic responses in advance—and keeping them linked to outcomes—you'll answer these questions with confidence and clarity. Remember, this part of the interview isn't about selling a flawless version of yourself. It's about showing who you really are, how you work, and where you're headed next.

How to Sell Yourself Without Feeling Pushy

Selling yourself in an interview isn't about bragging — it's about clearly showing the value you bring. Here's how to do it with authenticity and impact:

- **Focus on Value, Not Vanity** - Talk about the results you've achieved, the problems you've solved, or the way you've made others' jobs easier. Use numbers, feedback, and outcomes to support your points.

- **Tell Stories, Not Just Facts** - Use the STAR method (Situation, Task, Action, Result) to frame your experiences. Storytelling is memorable — and lets your strengths speak for themselves.

- **Align With What They Need** - Tailor your pitch to the role. Don't just list strengths; connect them directly to the company's challenges, goals, or culture.

- **Own Your Strengths with Confidence** - Say things like "One of the things I'm known for is..." or "Something I bring to every role is..." This softens the delivery but still shows confidence.

- **Let Others Vouch For You** - Mention feedback you've received: "My previous manager often said I was the go-to for solving client escalations."

- **Finish Strong** - End interviews or questions with a summary that reinforces your value: "That's why I believe I could really hit the ground running in this role."

You don't need to have a perfect answer for every question—but you do need to know your story. Common interview questions aren't just about ticking boxes; they're about showing the interviewer who you are and how you think. The more comfortable you are with your own experiences—even the unrelated ones—the easier it is to speak with confidence and purpose.

Own your journey. Know your value. That's what will make you stand out.

You've now got the tools to navigate the most common interview questions—those classics like *"Tell me about yourself"* or *"What are your strengths?"*—with clarity and intention. If you need more examples or want to practise your responses, head to the **Resources and Tools for Success** section. There you'll find sample answers, reframes, and prompts to help you fine-tune your approach.

But interviews don't stop at surface-level questions. The real insight—the part that helps hiring managers decide if you're the right fit—often comes when you're asked to talk about how you behave, think, and perform in real-world situations. This next chapter digs deeper. It's where we explore the behavioural and situational questions that show who you are through what you've done. We'll break down what these questions are really asking, how to structure your answers without sounding rehearsed, and how to turn your past experiences into compelling stories that stick.

Because when you can show—not just tell—how you handle pressure, lead teams, and solve problems, you don't just answer the question. You'll leave no doubt that you belong in the role.

Chapter Eight

Mastering Behavioural and Situational Questions

Demonstrating Who You Are Through What You've Done

Let's be honest—this is the chapter that could make all the difference in your interview. Because no matter how polished your résumé is or how well you've researched the company, if you can't clearly explain *how* you've done what you say you can do, you're going to lose momentum fast.

Key Points:

- Understand the Purpose: These questions are designed to reveal how you think, solve problems, and collaborate—not just your technical know-how.

- Use the STAR Method: It keeps your answers clear, focused, and easy to follow.

- Be Prepared with Real Examples: Have 5–7 strong, flexible stories that reflect your strengths.

- Avoid Generic or Scripted Responses: Show your thinking. Bring your answers to life with real context and reflection.

- Focus on Relevance and Growth: Choose stories that link to the role you're applying for—and be ready to share what you learned or how you've grown from the experience.

Behavioural and situational questions are some of the most important parts of any interview—and, are the ones people tend to stumble on the most. These aren't just throwaway questions. They're deliberately designed to uncover how you *think*, how you *respond* under pressure, and how you *work with others*. They're less about ticking off technical experience and more about revealing your mindset, your process, and your self-awareness.

But here's the thing: interviewers aren't looking for vague stories. They're not looking for something scripted or surface-level. And they definitely don't want to hear "I guess there was this one time..."

What they *do* want is specificity. They're asking for one clear moment in time—something real, with a beginning, middle, and end. They're listening for structure. For insight. For reflection. That's where your answers need to shine.

I always tell candidates: *generic isn't enough*. If I have to prompt someone in an interview, I'll often ask:

"Can you walk me through what you actually did?", "What was the outcome?" or "What did you learn?"

Because I'm looking for the *methodology* behind the story—not just the headline. Interviewers want to hear the thinking that sits underneath your actions. That's what gives your answer weight.

Why the STAR Method Works

This is where the STAR method comes in—and it's your best friend in answering these questions with clarity and confidence. It was developed in the 1980s as part of structured behavioural interviews—aimed at making hiring decisions fairer and more consistent by focusing on past performance as a reliable predictor of future behaviour. And it's still just as relevant today.

- **S – Situation**: Set the scene. What was happening? Where were you?

- **T – Task**: What was your role or objective? What needed to be done?

- **A – Action**: What steps did *you* take? This is the most important part—focus on what you contributed, not just what the team did.

- **R – Result**: What happened in the end? Did things improve? Did you learn something? Always tie it back to impact.

When you use STAR properly, your answer doesn't just tick boxes—it becomes a story with substance. A strong STAR response shows confidence, structure, and insight without feeling rehearsed or robotic.

What a Good STAR Response Sounds Like

Let's take a simple example and break it down:

"A customer was upset about a delayed shipment and couldn't get the information they needed online. I listened to their concerns, apologised for the inconvenience, and offered a discount on their next purchase. The customer

appreciated the gesture and continued shopping with us."

It's short. It's real. It shows empathy, initiative, and accountability. No fluff. That's STAR done well.

And here's the good news—your stories don't need to be earth-shattering. You don't need to have saved a business from collapse to make a great impression. You just need to choose examples that clearly show how you think and how you work. That's what employers are really listening for.

Behavioural vs Situational: What's the Difference?

A **behavioural** question usually starts with "Tell me about a time…" or "Give me an example of when…"
These are based on your *past* experiences.

A **situational** question is more hypothetical: "What would you do if…"
These explore how you *might* handle a future challenge.

But here's a trick: if you've faced something similar in the past, answer a situational question with a real-life story. Just say, "Actually, I've experienced something like this before—here's what I did." That makes your answer more compelling and grounded.

Be Strategic with Your Stories

You'll likely be asked more than one of these questions in a single interview. So variety matters. Having a mix of stories—covering things like conflict resolution, managing deadlines, working under pressure, leadership, learning from mistakes, and working in teams—gives you options. And remember: the *same story* can often be used in different ways, depending on the angle. It's about what part you focus on.

You don't need to memorise scripts—but you do need to be prepared. Think of your stories like tools in a toolkit. When the right question comes up, you know exactly which one to reach for.

And if you need help shaping your answers or figuring out what kinds of stories to tell, head to the ***Resources and Tools for Success*** section at the end of this book. I've included a list of behavioural and situational questions along with example responses you can use to guide your own prep. You can even use these to build your own story bank.

Most importantly—don't fall into the trap of treating these questions like a memory test. You're not being judged on your ability to rattle off a rehearsed script. You're being assessed on how well you can reflect, adapt, and communicate what matters. One of the biggest mistakes candidates make is defaulting to vague, impersonal answers that miss the mark. When I prompt someone to dig deeper in an interview, it's not because I'm trying to catch them out—it's because I know the value is there. I just need to see the thinking behind it.

So instead of saying "We worked as a team and got it done," tell me what *you* actually did. What made you step up? What changed because of your involvement? And what did you take away from the experience? These are the details that reveal who you are—not just what you've done. Even if it was a small task, if it shows initiative, insight, or growth, it matters. Especially in roles where problem-solving, communication, and ownership are critical.

Great answers don't happen by accident. They come from preparation, from reflecting on your past, and from taking the time to understand the value you bring. You don't need to be perfect—but, as I keep saying, you do need to be prepared. Because when you can communicate your impact with clarity and confidence, you don't just answer a question—you leave an impression that sticks.

Now, let's mix it up a bit. In the next chapter, we're going to talk about a part of the interview process that many people forget—your chance to ask questions. Because interviews are never just one-sided. They're a two-way street. And asking the right questions is a powerful way to find out whether the job—and the company—is actually right for you.

Chapter Nine
Asking Questions in Job Interviews
How Curiosity, Confidence and Clarity Help You Find the Right Fit

Interviews are often perceived as one-sided, with the interviewer driving the conversation and the candidate simply responding. However, I always remind candidates that interviews are a two-way street. While the interviewer is evaluating you, you should also be assessing the role, the company, and whether this is the right opportunity for you. Many candidates hesitate to ask questions during an interview, believing it might come across as overstepping or unprepared. In reality, asking thoughtful questions demonstrates confidence, curiosity, and genuine interest in the role and company.

Key Points:
- Gain clarity on the role and expectations.

- Understand the company culture and values.

- Determine if the position aligns with your career goals and address potential concerns before accepting an offer.

- Remember, an interview isn't just about impressing the employer; it's about ensuring the role is a good fit for you.

Setting the Tone Early

At the start of the interview, it's a good idea to express your gratitude and enthusiasm while setting the stage for a two-way conversation. You might say something like: "Thank you so much for your time today. I'm really excited to answer your questions about my résumé and experience. If it's okay, I've prepared a few questions myself. Would it be alright to ask those at the end if we have time? If not, I'd be happy to send them through as a follow-up." This approach demonstrates professionalism, preparedness, and respect for the interviewer's time while signalling your genuine interest in the role.

Shikha's Story Continued

Shikha's experience is a perfect example of why asking the right questions matters. During one of our prep sessions, she expressed frustration about past interviews where she missed opportunities to gain clarity because she didn't know how to frame her questions or felt uncomfortable asking them. For her upcoming interview, she was applying for a casual role but wanted to know if it could transition into a permanent position. She wasn't sure how to approach this without sounding too direct.

I suggested framing it like this: "Given that this role is casual, I'd like to know if there's an opportunity for it to become permanent. Have you had instances where casual roles have transitioned to permanent positions in the past? If so, how did that happen?"

Another concern was her lack of information about the hiring manager, as she had only been provided a name. She wanted to learn about their background and leadership style but was unsure how to ask without seeming intrusive. I advised her to take a conversational approach, such as: "I noticed you've been with the company for a while. What drew you to this role, and what's kept you here? Can you tell me about how you got the role and what skills you've developed?"

By preparing these questions in advance, Shikha not only gained confidence but also demonstrated to the interviewer that she was proactive and genuinely interested in the role.

As the interview prep wrapped up, I encouraged her to ask two more powerful questions—something many candidates hesitate to do but more experienced, seasoned candidates have no hesitation in asking:

> "Is there anything I haven't outlined in my experience or on my résumé or do you have any reason I wouldn't be suitable for the role?"

Years ago, candidates were more direct in asking for the job or for next steps but now there seems to be uncertainty with getting feedback. These questions, though simple, are incredibly effective but it's finding the balance of coming across too confident and genuine interest. They also aren't uncommon questions but are more common with senior and experienced candidates (George, in Chapter Twelve, told me he asked these questions at the end of his interviews over twenty years ago - by asking, he got live feedback and the role).

It shows you're open to feedback, gives you a chance to clarify or expand on anything that may not have landed well, and shows the interviewer that you're self-aware and willing to improve. It also allows you to walk away from the interview with confidence, knowing you've left no stone unturned.

Asking Questions of Recruiters

Recruiters are often the first point of contact in the hiring process. Their role is to evaluate a candidate's suitability for a position, but they should also provide valuable insights into the company and help prepare candidates for interviews.

A strong recruiter does more than fill roles—they align candidates with positions that fit their skills, goals, and personality. My approach is to not match a résumé to a position description but to genuinely find the right fit for both the client and the candidate.

When meeting with a recruiter, don't hesitate to ask them detailed questions. They should also help you decide whether the position is right for you.

Case Study: The $250K Interview Without Preparation

A friend of mine, a seasoned executive, recently went through a process for a senior role paying over $250,000. The recruiter—who had been in the industry for years—offered minimal guidance leading up to her panel interview with four board members. She wasn't sent a position description, only the original job ad and a link to the company's website.

The day before the interview, the recruiter mentioned it would be a panel format with 10 prepared questions—but wouldn't share those questions in advance. Despite her experience and professionalism, she felt underprepared. While the interview itself went smoothly, the lack of guidance made her doubt both the recruiter and the company's internal structure.

Post-interview, she had to chase the recruiter for feedback. He was vague and didn't follow up until Sunday, eventually confirming a second interview—details he should have known well in advance. That second interview consisted of nearly identical questions to the first, which felt like a waste of time, especially after a two-hour drive. To top it off, she bumped into the other candidate while having coffee with potential team members.

This experience highlights a critical takeaway: not all recruiters offer strategic preparation, even at executive levels.

Areas to Explore When Asking Questions

Instead of simply asking for the sake of it, think about the purpose behind your questions. Each one should give you greater clarity on whether this is the right move for you—not just in terms of the job, but also the people, culture, and long-term alignment.

- **Career Progression** - Understanding what growth looks like within the company gives you insight into how your career could evolve. It helps you assess whether there's a clear path for development, or if the role may become stagnant after the initial responsibilities are mastered.

- **Learning About the Hiring Manager** - The person you report to has a massive influence on your day-to-day experience. Asking questions that help you understand their management style, communication preferences, and leadership approach can help you determine if it's someone you'll work well with—or not.

- **Setting Expectations** - Knowing what success looks like early on is critical. When a company can clearly articulate expectations for your first few months, it shows that they've thought about the role strategically. It also gives you a target to work toward if you're successful.

- **Measuring Success** - Beyond initial expectations, it's important to understand how your performance will be evaluated long term. This helps you understand the company's priorities and whether their version of "success" aligns with your own.

- **Team Dynamics and Culture** - Culture is more than just a buzzword—it affects everything from how decisions are made to how people support each other under pressure. Ask questions that help you picture yourself working with the team. Do they value collaboration, or is it more siloed? Are they high-pressure or relaxed? These nuances matter.

- **History and Story - Understanding background.** If you're speaking with the business owner or founder, learning their 'why' can reveal what drives the company. Their passion, purpose, and long-term vision may resonate with you—or it might raise red flags if it doesn't align with your values or career goals.

- **Competitiveness** - Understanding how many candidates are in the process gives you insight into the timeline and intensity of the competition. It also helps you gauge whether you're in early stages or at final shortlist.

- **Timeframe** - These questions help you understand urgency and readiness. If they don't have a start date in mind or an onboarding plan in place, it could be a sign of poor planning or internal disorganisation.

- **Knowing the Next Steps** - It's essential to leave the interview knowing what happens next. Clear next steps reflect a well-structured process and reduce anxiety during the waiting period.

- **Feedback** - A company's willingness to offer feedback—regardless of outcome—demonstrates transparency and professionalism. It's also a sign they value the candidate experience.

Each area of questioning—such as understanding career progression, the hiring manager's style, performance expectations, team culture, and onboarding—serves to provide a fuller picture of the company and the role you're walking into. These conversations help you avoid surprises, uncover dealbreakers, and decide if the opportunity truly fits.

A full list of sample questions is provided in ***Resources and Tools for Success*** so you can prepare thoughtfully and adapt your questions to suit different interview formats and stages.

Interviews Are Conversations, Not Exams

Shikha's journey showed us how preparation and thoughtful questioning can build confidence, demonstrate engagement, and uncover vital details about the opportunity at hand.

At the other end of the scale, the executive case study from earlier in this chapter reminds us that even the most senior professionals can be left in the dark if the recruiter—and the company—aren't proactive or transparent. When recruiters fail to provide even the basics, it's more than just a poor experience—it's often a signal of deeper issues. A lack of communication or clarity during the recruitment process can reflect how the company operates internally and how it treats its people once they're on board. It's a reminder that red flags aren't limited to junior-level roles; they can appear at any stage, and paying attention to them matters—regardless of your experience level.

So, what can we learn from both?

Never assume
Whether you're an entry-level applicant or a seasoned executive, never assume that the recruiter or company has covered everything you need to know. Details about the role, expectations, timelines, or even who you're meeting with can be missed. If something isn't clear—ask. Clear information leads to confident preparation.

Always ask
Asking thoughtful questions shows initiative and helps uncover details that might otherwise be overlooked. From understanding the company culture to clarifying expectations around performance or onboarding, questions empower you to make informed decisions—and they often reveal just as much about the employer as they do about the role.

Treat every interaction as a two-way conversation
Interviews, phone calls, emails—every exchange is an opportunity to assess fit on both sides. It's not just about impressing the employer; it's also about deciding whether this is the right environment for you. Pay attention to how you're treated, how clearly things are communicated, and whether your time and questions are respected. These early signs can be incredibly telling.

Asking thoughtful questions isn't about being difficult or demanding—it's about protecting your time, your career, and your peace of mind. It's how you take back control in a process that can often feel uncertain.

Whether you're sitting across from a recruiter, a hiring manager, or a founder, your questions reflect your priorities, your preparedness, and your professionalism.

No matter how many questions you prepare, the format of the interview can still throw you off if you're not ready for it. Virtual interviews—Zoom, Teams, Google Meet—are now a standard step in most recruitment processes. And while they offer convenience and accessibility, they also bring a new layer of challenge when it comes to presence, body language, and connection.

In the next chapter, we'll explore how to bring your best self into digital spaces, create strong rapport through a screen, and navigate the tech side of things without stress. Whether it's your first virtual interview or your fiftieth, I'll walk you through exactly how to prepare, present, and perform with confidence.

Chapter Ten
Mastering Virtual Interviews
The Importance of Preparation

Virtual interviews are now a standard part of the hiring process. In today's world—shaped by remote work, digital-first interactions, and increasingly global hiring practices—video interviews are often your first real opportunity to make an impression. And while they may seem more casual or convenient than in-person meetings, don't underestimate their weight. For many employers, your virtual presence is their first insight into how you communicate, present yourself, and respond under pressure.

Whether you're chatting with a recruiter, meeting a panel via Zoom, or joining a future manager on Microsoft Teams, how you show up on screen can be just as powerful—if not more so—than a firm handshake across a desk. I've met some of the most incredible candidates through video interviews—but I've also seen exceptional résumés fall flat due to poor lighting, distracting backgrounds, or technical glitches. It's not just about being seen and heard. *It's about how* you're seen and heard.

Key Points:

- Virtual interviews are now standard across most industries.

- Your video presence is often the first impression you make.

- Casual preparation can leave a lasting (and not always positive) mark.

- A strong virtual setup reflects professionalism, adaptability, and initiative.

The Importance of Setup

Virtual interview prep goes beyond rehearsing responses or researching the company. It includes setting up your technical and physical environment.

Camera – Keep it at eye level and centred on your face. Avoid looking down at your screen or up at the ceiling—it breaks the sense of connection. Test your framing and resolution the day before, if possible.

Background – Your space matters. If you're working from a messy bedroom or have a visible kitchen sink behind you, use the "blur" or virtual background function. Even better, choose a tidy, neutral space that doesn't steal focus.

Lighting – Natural light is ideal, but if that's not an option, use a soft lamp facing your face. Avoid sitting with your back to a window unless you're going for the "mysterious silhouette" look (not recommended).

Audio – You'd be surprised how often candidates talk for 10 minutes before realising they're inaudible. Use headphones or a reliable mic, test your setup in advance, and have a backup plan ready.

Adapting to the Interviewer's Setup

Not all interviewers will have perfect setups either. If the connection drops, their audio cuts out, or you can't hear clearly—*say something*. Staying silent helps no one.

Polite clarification shows your professionalism and keeps things on track. Try:

"Sorry, I didn't quite catch that—would you mind repeating the question?"

or

"Just checking—did my last response come through clearly?"

It's not about being flawless. It's about handling issues with calm and confidence. Glitches, lags, and background noise happen to everyone—including the person interviewing you. Addressing them with ease shows you're adaptable, composed, and easy to work with.

Using a Phone for a Virtual Interview

Yes, sometimes phone-based video interviews are necessary—especially in sales, field roles, or trades where access to a laptop isn't always possible.

If that's the case, **communicate it upfront**:

"Just letting you know—I'll be taking the call from my phone due to work commitments, but I'll ensure I'm in a quiet, professional space."

Phones are fine. But *phone-in-hand, walking through a carpark while dodging traffic and yelling over background noise*? Absolutely not.

Be conscious of your surroundings. If it's less than ideal, acknowledge it briefly and stay calm and present. Professionalism isn't about fancy tech—it's about how you manage the moment.

Soft Skills Still Matter

Non-verbal communication carries more weight than you think—even on video. The camera may mute some nuance, but how you hold yourself, speak, and engage still tells a story.

- **Engagement** – Look at the camera (not your own video feed), nod occasionally, smile when appropriate, and show you're listening.

- **Body Language** – Sit upright, avoid fidgeting, and lean in slightly when speaking or listening.

- **Voice** – Speak clearly, vary your tone, and avoid mumbling or trailing off. Confidence comes through in your delivery—even over shaky Wi-Fi.

The Risks of Poor Preparation

Neglecting your virtual setup doesn't just impact your first impression—it can completely derail the conversation. Common risks include:

- **Miscommunication** – Background noise or a poor connection can make you miss questions or render your answers unclear.

- **Distraction** – A cluttered room or unexpected interruption might be more memorable than your experience.

- **Missed Opportunities** – Technical issues or lack of eye contact can quietly erode trust and overshadow your strengths.

Case Study: When the Setup Undermined the Interview

Here's a real-life example of how poor virtual setup—despite great intent—can throw off the entire interview.

I once interviewed a candidate for an accounts officer role. Over the phone, he was fantastic: engaging, friendly, and genuinely enthusiastic.

He confirmed the time and said he'd be there "with bells on." I was really looking forward to meeting him.

But as the video interview started, things quickly fell apart.

He had trouble connecting, even though our email outlined the link and instructions. After dropping off, he rejoined via phone—which was fine. But his camera was pointed at the ceiling, revealing only water stains and the top of his head. Occasionally, I'd catch a glimpse of his nose.

I asked him a few times to adjust his camera, but the audio was patchy and it was clear he couldn't hear me. The tech setup became the focus—and not just for me. It affected his ability to connect as well.

The role was remote, requiring regular video calls with both the team and clients. In the end, despite his résumé and phone manner, I didn't progress him. Not because he used a phone—but because the setup showed a lack of preparation and created disconnection.

This wasn't about being perfect. It was about *effort*. And unfortunately, the takeaway wasn't professionalism—it was a missed opportunity.

Overcoming Common Challenges

Things go wrong. That's life. But it's how you handle those moments that matters most.

Stay calm. Own the issue. "Apologies for the noise—just one moment while I mute and sort it out."

Have a backup. Provide your mobile number in advance in case the video drops out.

Minimise disruptions. Give your housemates a heads-up. Lock the dog out. Stick a note on the front door.

It's not about creating a perfect bubble—it's about showing that you've *thought ahead*.

Tech Tips & Tools

- **Know the platform** – Zoom, Teams, Google Meet—get familiar, especially with screen sharing and muting.

- **Upgrade (if you can)** – A $30 ring light, a basic headset, and a laptop stand go a long way.

- **Have a Plan B** – If your internet drops, switch to mobile data or call the interviewer directly.

Why It All Matters

Your virtual presence is a reflection of how you approach your work. It shows whether you prepare, take initiative, and understand the expectations of modern roles—especially remote or hybrid ones.

When your tech is sorted, your space is calm, and your energy is present, you give your strengths room to shine. You're not trying to be perfect. You're trying to be *prepared*. And that's what sets you apart.

This level of intention tells your future employer something important: you care about how you show up.

In a virtual world full of distractions and blurred boundaries, consistency and professionalism matter more than ever.

Mastering virtual interviews is one thing—but what happens when the interview itself throws you a curveball?
Maybe it's a group assessment. Maybe it's a panel. Or you're asked to role-play, complete a test, or handle a challenge on the spot.

These are the moments that separate the prepared from the truly adaptable.

Interviews are never just about what's said—they're about what's experienced. And in a virtual world, the environment you create becomes part of that experience.

In the next chapter, we'll dive into Adapting to Different and Challenging Interview Types—from panels to presentations, technical tasks to culture-fit scenarios. You'll learn how to handle them with poise, presence, and a plan.

Chapter Eleven

Adapting to Different and Challenging Interview Types

Strategies for Handling Every Interview Format with Confidence

You won't always walk into a quiet room with one person across the table and a glass of water waiting for you. Interviews today come in many shapes—from phone calls taken on your lunch break, to virtual panels with six faces on a screen. Each format brings a different energy, and the key to handling them is knowing what to expect and how to show up.

Key Points:

- Tailor your approach to the interview type—know what's expected.

- Preparation builds confidence, especially when facing unfamiliar formats.

- Understand what's legally appropriate to be asked—and what's not.

- Stay composed under pressure to make a strong impression.

Types of Interviews and How to Navigate Them

Phone Interviews

Often used as an initial screening step, phone interviews are designed to confirm basic qualifications, availability, and communication skills. Without the benefit of facial expressions or body language, the emphasis shifts to your tone, clarity, and active listening. Keep your answers concise, smile while you speak (it comes through in your voice), and have your résumé and notes in front of you for reference.

Pro Tip: Take the call in a quiet space, use a headset if possible, and have a glass of water nearby. This keeps your voice clear and your hands free to jot down notes.

One-on-One (In-Person) Interviews

Still a staple in many hiring processes, this format allows for a deeper personal connection. These interviews focus less on group dynamics and more on rapport, communication, and your ability to articulate your value clearly. Stay present, build trust, and show curiosity about the role and company.

Panel Interviews

In a panel interview, you'll meet with multiple interviewers at once—sometimes from different departments. These can occur at any stage and are often used in high-volume or collaborative roles. Make a point to engage with each person, address their questions directly, and maintain inclusive eye contact. Don't be thrown if one panel member is quieter or more intense—stay balanced and professional throughout.

Pro Tip: Remember names or job titles, if possible. Address people respectfully and equally, even if one is clearly "leading" the interview.

Behind the Scenes: What I've Seen in Panels and Assessments

I've sat on both sides of the table during panel interviews—and in my experience, candidates who stay calm, acknowledge everyone in the room, and adapt to shifting energy leave a lasting impression. It's not about having perfect answers; it's about *connecting* with each person, even briefly, and showing that you can stay composed in a more layered environment.

I've also designed and run assessment centres for graduate programs and volume hires. These are often high-pressure, structured days with role plays, team tasks, and time-bound presentations. What stands out isn't who talks the loudest—it's who contributes meaningfully, reads the room, and supports others while staying authentic. The best candidates? They balance visibility with humility, and they walk in prepared but not over-rehearsed.

Group Interviews

Used to evaluate how candidates interact with others, group interviews are common in customer service, retail, graduate programs, and high-turnover industries. You might be asked to participate in group activities or answer questions alongside other candidates—designed to test your ability to collaborate while still standing out. Speak up clearly, support others' input when appropriate, and find natural moments to add value without dominating the conversation.

Case Interviews

Popular in consulting, analytics, and technical roles, case interviews focus on your problem-solving process. You'll be asked to work through a hypothetical scenario or real-world business problem under time pressure. These interviews assess not just your solution, but how you arrive at it—your logic, structure, and clarity of thought.

Pro Tip: Talk through your thought process out loud. Employers are listening for how you approach uncertainty and organise complex ideas.

Virtual Interviews

Virtual interviews have become a normal part of the hiring process, not just a pandemic workaround. They're used at every stage and often carry the same weight as in-person meetings. Test your technology beforehand, use a neutral and well-lit background, and eliminate distractions. Maintain eye contact by looking at the camera, not the screen, and speak with clear intention.

Pro Tip: Dress professionally from head to toe. It impacts your mindset and sets you up the right way.

Adaptability is Your Advantage

Being able to shift gears between different interview types is a powerful asset. Employers are looking for candidates who can stay composed, read the room, and communicate clearly regardless of the format. Every setting is a chance to showcase not only your technical skills but also your adaptability and emotional intelligence.

Understanding Dynamics Across Locations and Decision-Makers

While interview formats shape how you prepare, the people conducting them—and the context in which interviews take place—can have an equally significant impact. Even within the same organisation, interviews can differ wildly between locations, departments, or hiring managers. The following case study illustrates how these inconsistencies can influence not only your experience but also the outcome.

Case Study: When the Location Shapes the Outcome - Interviewing Across Locations or Departments

Alex applied for a role at a national recruitment firm, initially interviewing with a friendly HR representative at the head office in Brisbane. The position, though within the IT division, was not one he had direct experience in—but the HR team saw potential and supported his application for a second-stage interview with the department head based at the Gold Coast office.

The second interview was vastly different. The interviewer arrived late and displayed disinterested body language from the outset. Despite the role being in IT, most of the questions focused on Alex's unrelated experience in construction and hospitality. His relevant procurement and BDM experience—directly aligned with the advertised role—was overlooked. The interviewer scribbled across his CV without context, made minimal eye contact, and offered no time for Alex to ask questions. The entire interview wrapped up in under 30 minutes.

Alex later found out, via HR, that the interviewer claimed he had sworn during the conversation—a statement Alex strongly denied. He was also informed that the hiring manager historically favoured a specific candidate profile—"tall, blonde, surfie types"—suggesting a culture of bias that had little to do with capability.

This experience highlights an often-overlooked challenge in the interview process: inconsistencies across different locations or hiring managers within the same company. Even when one part of the organisation values your potential, bias or misalignment at the team level can derail your chances. It also reflects the importance of post-interview follow-up and self-advocacy—Alex only discovered the fabricated feedback after reaching out himself.

Pro Tip: If you're progressing through multi-stage interviews with different people or at different locations (including virtual sites), try to get clarity upfront about who you'll be meeting, what their role is, and how their team operates. This not only helps you prepare relevant questions, but also allows you to tailor your examples and responses to each person's priorities and perspective.

Ask the initial interviewer or recruiter questions like:

- "Can you tell me a bit about the person I'll be meeting with next?"

- "What's their role in the hiring process?"

- "Is there anything I should know about their leadership style, or how they prefer to communicate?"

These kinds of questions demonstrate professionalism and initiative—and they give you helpful insights into the team dynamics and company culture.

And remember: if something feels off—whether it's a vague answer, a disorganised schedule, or inconsistent communication—it's okay to ask for clarification. You can also share your concerns with the original recruiter or contact point. You're not being difficult; you're being thoughtful about where you invest your time and energy.

How a company treats you during the interview process is a powerful preview of how they'll treat you once you're on the team. Pay attention—it's not just about impressing them; it's also about protecting your own values, time, and career direction.

Summary & Key Takeaways:

Interview styles vary widely—knowing what to expect helps you stay composed.
From one-on-one chats to panels, group assessments to technical evaluations, interview formats can shift quickly. The more familiar you are with different styles, the easier it is to stay focused, adapt your communication, and bring your best self to each stage.

Not all interviewers are trained or unbiased; know when to advocate for yourself.
Sometimes, you'll encounter interviewers who are underprepared, distracted, or even unaware of the role details. In rare cases, bias or poor conduct can slip in. If something feels off, trust your instincts—advocating for yourself doesn't mean being difficult; it means being clear and professional about your needs and boundaries.

Be proactive in asking questions and clarifying role expectations across locations.
Especially in multi-stage or multi-site processes, don't assume consistency. Ask about team structures, reporting lines, and how decisions are made.

The more you know, the more confidently you can speak to how you'd fit into their world.

Watch for red flags in body language, organisation, or interviewer conduct.
Interviews are a two-way mirror. Notice how prepared the interviewer is, how they treat your time, and whether their behaviour aligns with the company's stated values. A disorganised process, dismissive tone, or lack of follow-through can indicate bigger cultural issues.

If necessary, follow up post-interview to seek clarity and protect your reputation.
If something was unclear or didn't sit right with you, it's okay to circle back respectfully. A quick follow-up email to your recruiter or main contact can provide clarity, reinforce your professionalism, and help ensure your side of the story is heard—especially in more complex processes.

Legal and Ethical Considerations in Interviews

Some interviews—particularly for roles in education, healthcare, community services, or trades—may include questions about physical capacity or legal clearances. These questions are valid only when they relate directly to the inherent requirements of the job. It's not just about what an employer wants to know—it's about what they're legally allowed to ask.

For example, an employer can legally ask: *"This role requires lifting up to 20kg. Are you able to meet this requirement?"* This is a fair and job-relevant question, as it relates to physical duties required for safe job performance.

However, they cannot ask: *"Do you have any injuries, back issues, or medical conditions?"* This type of question crosses into protected personal information and could breach anti-discrimination laws. It's a subtle but important difference: employers can ask about your ability to perform a task—not your personal health history.

In Australia, workplace health and safety regulations (WHS) also guide what's considered a reasonable physical requirement. Manual handling expectations can start at around 16kg depending on the industry and role, and employers must ensure any physical tasks align with safe work practices and are clearly communicated from the outset.

Similarly, if a role involves working with children, elderly people, or other vulnerable groups, it is reasonable for an employer to ask if you are willing to undergo a Working with Children Check or a police check. These checks are standard in many sectors and are used to ensure the safety of those being supported.

Importantly, in Australia, any background checks—whether criminal history, working rights, or physical capacity—must be directly tied to the job's core duties. These expectations should be outlined in job advertisements, position descriptions, or early in the recruitment process. If they're not clear, you are well within your rights to ask for clarification before proceeding.

If you're ever asked a question that feels invasive, discriminatory, or irrelevant, you have options. You can politely redirect by asking how the question relates to the role, or you can raise concerns with the recruiter or employer post-interview.

Keeping calm, professional, and informed in these moments allows you to protect your rights while still advocating for yourself with confidence.

Examples of Illegal Interview Questions

Under anti-discrimination laws, the following questions are off-limits:

- "How old are you?"
- "Are you married or do you have children?"
- "What religion do you practice?"
- "Do you have any health conditions?"
- "Are you pregnant?"
- "Where were you born?"
- "Have you ever been arrested?"

These questions have no bearing on your ability to do the job. If you're asked one, you have every right to redirect, decline to answer, or follow up later if needed.

How to Handle Inappropriate Questions

You may not want to confront the interviewer directly, especially in the moment. Here are a few graceful ways to respond:

- **Politely Redirect:** "I'm not sure how that relates to the role, but I'd be happy to share more about my experience managing similar projects."
- **Ask for Clarification:** "Could you clarify how that question connects to the responsibilities of the role?"
- **Give a General Answer:** "I believe my skills and experience make me well-suited to this position, and I'm focused on bringing strong outcomes to the team."

- **Maintain Poise:** Even if you're surprised or uncomfortable, take a breath and respond with calm confidence.

- **Follow Up Later:** If the question felt inappropriate or discriminatory, you may choose to raise it with HR or a relevant authority. You are under no obligation to tolerate illegal or invasive questioning.

Journal Prompt: Think back to any interview or professional setting where you felt a question was too personal. How did you respond, and what would you do differently with this knowledge?

Acceptable Job-Related Questions

Some questions are perfectly reasonable—when they relate to the core functions of the job. Examples include:

- "Are you able to work weekend shifts on a rotating roster?"
- "Do you hold a current Working with Children Check?"
- "Do you have a valid driver's licence?"
- "Are you physically able to stand for extended periods or lift heavy objects?"

If you're unsure whether a certain question is appropriate, ask yourself: Does this relate directly to performing the role? If not, you're not required to answer.

Handling Tough Interview Scenarios

Even the most prepared candidate will hit a curveball now and then. These moments can feel uncomfortable—but they're also an opportunity to show grace under pressure. How you respond when things go off-script can leave a lasting impression, often more than a perfectly rehearsed answer.

If You Don't Know the Answer

It's okay not to have every answer on the spot. What matters is how you handle it. Own it honestly, and then pivot with purpose.

Try something like: "That's a great question. I'm not sure off the top of my head, but here's how I would approach finding the answer…"

This shows you're not flustered, but rather thoughtful and resourceful. You're demonstrating critical thinking and initiative—qualities that are far more valuable than memorised facts.

You can also share a relevant framework or process you'd use to solve the problem. This not only keeps the conversation moving but also shows how you tackle uncertainty with confidence and a plan.

Résumé Gaps or Career Changes

Whether your gap was due to caregiving, study, health, travel, or reassessing your career direction, your experience is valid—and it's part of your story.

Speak to it with calm confidence: "During that time, I focused on [developing new skills / caring for family / upskilling / recovering from a health issue], and I'm now ready to bring fresh energy into my next role."

The key here is to highlight what you gained, not just what you paused.

Interviewers want to see your motivation and readiness—not an apology for time away. By showing that you've reflected, grown, and developed during that time, you shift the narrative from a "gap" to a period of purposeful growth.

Addressing a Difficult Past Role or Manager

Avoid speaking poorly of former colleagues or managers—even if the situation was genuinely tough. Instead, focus on what the experience taught you: "It was a challenging environment, but it helped me strengthen my communication and boundary-setting skills. I learned a lot about what kind of leadership I thrive under." This approach shows maturity and emotional intelligence. You're acknowledging the reality without bitterness—and redirecting the focus onto how you've evolved and what you're now looking for in a workplace.

To succeed in any interview, it's essential to adapt to the style and format by understanding expectations and preparing accordingly. Equally important is knowing your rights—illegal questions are off-limits, and you're never obligated to answer them. Challenging moments during interviews are inevitable, but they can be opportunities to demonstrate your professionalism, flexibility, and resilience. The more interviews you navigate, the more confident and capable you become at handling different formats and situations. As you become more comfortable with these, you'll find it easier to transition into second-round interviews. These often involve new decision-makers, deeper questions, or even presentations—and require a more refined, strategic approach.

The next chapter explores exactly that. Second interviews are a pivotal moment in the hiring process—a chance to elevate your candidacy and truly stand out from the competition. Unlike the first interview, which typically assesses your qualifications and cultural fit, the second interview delves deeper into your potential contributions and how well you align with the company's goals.

Chapter Twelve
Second Interview Strategies
Turning Interest Into Intent – Mastering the Next Stage

The second interview marks a significant shift in the hiring process. It's no longer just about your qualifications – it's about whether you're the *right fit* for the team, the culture, and the challenges ahead. It's your moment to step forward confidently, address any lingering questions, and show how you'll add value from day one. You're no longer a possibility – you're a serious contender.

Key Points:

- Clarify next steps early: Ask during the phone screen or first interview if there's a second stage and what it involves.

- Prepare for new faces and deeper questions: Expect to meet other stakeholders and go beyond surface-level answers.

- Think like a team member: Speak as if you're already part of the business – offer ideas and align your experience with their goals.

- Ask sharp, strategic questions: Show genuine interest by asking about priorities, culture, or upcoming challenges.

Second Interviews: A Deeper Evaluation

Second interviews are becoming increasingly common, especially for roles that involve greater responsibility, collaboration, or specialised expertise. Employers use this stage to assess how you'll fit within the team, how you think, and how you approach real-world challenges. More than just a formality, this stage allows both the employer and candidate to test for alignment—values, communication style, and vision.

> "I've always encouraged the use of second interviews, as they offer an invaluable chance to clarify expectations on both sides."

Done well, they help employers visualise you in the role—and help you determine if this is where you truly want to be. Your goal? Show up prepared, confident, and ready to elevate the conversation.

The Purpose of the Second Interview

Unlike the first interview, which covers capability and broad fit, the second interview dives into how you'll operate in their real-world environment. It's about the "how" behind your experience—how you interact, problem-solve, collaborate, and contribute to business goals. Employers are looking for someone who can not only *do the job*, but thrive in their particular context.

Hiring managers at this stage are assessing problem-solving ability, emotional intelligence, and growth potential. They're evaluating how your experience aligns with what's needed now—and what will be needed in the months ahead. This is your chance to prove that you understand their priorities and that you'll make a meaningful, measurable impact.

How to Prepare

As mentioned in earlier case studies, second interviews can be inconsistent—sometimes disorganised, repetitive, or completely different in tone. *Be ready to adapt.* Start by revisiting everything you've learned so far: what the employer shared in the first interview, any documentation they've provided (like the position description or company strategy), and your own notes. Also, if you know who will be on the panel or in the room, research their roles. It's a great way to anticipate the kinds of questions or concerns they might bring to the table.

Prepare to go deeper into your achievements and work style, and rehearse stories that showcase your contribution under pressure, in teams, and in uncertain situations. A well-structured story can make you unforgettable. This is your chance to bring your experience to life and show exactly how you've handled real challenges—something a CV alone can't capture.

As mentioned in Chapter Ten, use the **STAR method—Situation, Task, Action, Result**—to communicate your examples with clarity and impact. If you need a refresher, revisit Chapter Eight, where we explore this framework in depth and break down how to master behavioural interview questions.

Choose stories that closely align with the responsibilities and challenges of the role you're interviewing for. The goal is to help the interviewer *visualise you in the role*, solving problems, contributing to the team, and handling pressure like a pro.

You don't need to re-ask what's already been covered—this is your moment to ask thoughtful, strategic questions that show curiosity and initiative. If you've had time to reflect since your first interview, bring in new ideas or insights.

You might ask:

- What would success look like in the first 3–6 months?

- What challenges is the team currently facing?

- How do you see this role evolving over the next year?

This shifts the tone from "candidate" to "future colleague."

When Second Interviews Go Too Far

A Case Study in Bias, Process, and Knowing When to Walk Away

Let me share a real story—one that highlights why understanding the recruitment process early on is essential. We'll call him George.

George was referred for a corporate role by a friend in management. He was transitioning from a construction background and had solid experience. His first interview went well. The second was promising. But then came a third... and a fourth... and a fifth. In total, George went through **seven interviews** for the same role.

At first, the process seemed standard: two initial phone screens with internal recruitment, followed by interviews with two or three different managers. Then, a final panel interview with all managers, including the most senior decision-maker—who ultimately voted against hiring him.

The feedback? Vague. No real reason was provided, but later conversations revealed that this manager had taken a strong stance against George's appointment. Despite being competent, likeable, and well-prepared, he "just didn't feel like the right fit"—a phrase that often masks unconscious bias.

George's friend and manager, who eventually overrode that decision, believed there was **cultural or conscious bias** at play. George himself has reflected on this, acknowledging that his confident presence and background may have led some to perceive him as intimidating. He's worked hard since then to reshape that narrative—not by changing himself, but by proving his value through action.

That same senior manager left the company three months later. Since then, George not only replaced her but has been promoted further and now leads a large team—one that hasn't had a single resignation in the past three years.

Red Flags That Emerged

This case highlights several critical points:

- Excessive interviews indicate a lack of process - Seven interviews for a mid-level role suggest poor structure and indecision from the employer.

- Panel interviews can sometimes expose internal conflict - When a senior leader dominates or uses panels to validate personal biases, it creates confusion and mistrust.

- Unconscious bias can be hard to name, but easy to feel - Vague feedback or repeated delays may hint at discomfort with your background, presentation, or even just your confidence.

- No clear feedback is a red flag - If the only reason you're given is "not the right fit" with no examples or follow-up, that's not feedback—it's avoidance.

George's journey is a testament to resilience, clarity of self-worth, and the importance of knowing when to question a flawed process—but also when to stay the course if you believe in the role and the business.

Panel Interviews and How to Handle Them

If the second stage involves a panel, your job is to balance clarity with connection. Make eye contact with everyone, not just the person who asked the question. Be aware of body language—both yours and theirs—and read the room. Anticipate questions from different angles: one may focus on your technical skills, another on culture fit, leadership potential, or how you've handled conflict.

It's also common for panel members to have different levels of involvement with the role. One may be your future manager, while another might represent a cross-functional department or HR. Tailoring your responses to acknowledge those differences shows emotional intelligence and helps you build rapport across the table. If a panel member seems more reserved, don't overlook them—draw them in by referencing shared goals or asking a clarifying question that shows you value their perspective.

Preparation goes a long way here. Practise giving clear, structured responses that are still conversational. Think of each question as an opportunity to build trust—not just to prove what you know, but to show how you'll collaborate with different personalities and stakeholders.

Addressing Red Flags

Second interviews often dig into the grey areas—gaps in employment, career shifts, or even perceived over-qualification. If something's likely to raise a question, own it. Reframe it as an advantage: how it's helped you grow, what it taught you, and why it's made you even more ready for this role.

Anticipating these questions doesn't mean you're defending yourself—it means you're stepping into the conversation with confidence and honesty. The key is to avoid being overly apologetic or vague. Instead, give a clear and positive narrative that connects your past to your present with purpose. When you're prepared to speak to these areas with maturity and clarity, you turn potential question marks into compelling strengths.

Ending Strong

The way you close matters. Summarise your fit, reaffirm your interest, and thank them for the opportunity. You want to leave them thinking, *"They're ready."* A strong closing statement reinforces your enthusiasm and professionalism—and it helps you stay top of mind when the final decision is being made.

Your closing doesn't need to be scripted—it just needs to be confident and clear. And if you've taken the time to prepare a 90-day plan, your final moments in the interview can tie it all together. Show them you're not just ready to start—you're ready to make a meaningful impact.

A Strategy That Sets You Apart: The 90-Day Plan

If you truly want to elevate your second interview performance, one of the most effective tools you can use is a 90-day plan. I often get my candidates to prepare one in advance of the second interview—especially if I know it's coming (and I always should!). This is your opportunity to map out how you'd approach the role from day one, offering insight into your mindset, your work ethic, and your understanding of the company's needs.

And while 90-day plans are often associated with sales or leadership roles, their impact goes far beyond that. Junior professionals, admin staff, marketing grads—anyone stepping into a new environment—can benefit from thinking strategically about how they'll listen, learn, and contribute early on. It's not just about outlining tasks; it's about showing you're already imagining yourself in the role and taking ownership of your path forward.

This simple framework demonstrates initiative, clarity, and accountability—qualities that leave a lasting impression. It's one thing to say "I'm excited about the opportunity." It's another to show exactly how you plan to make the most of it.

Which brings us to one of the most powerful tools you can bring into a second interview—especially if you want to stand out for all the right reasons.

Chapter Thirteen
The 90-Day Plan
The Power of a 90-Day Plan in a Second Interview

As you prepare for a second interview, expectations are naturally higher. The hiring team knows you have the right experience and skills for the role, but now, they want to understand what you will do with them. A well-thought-out 90-day plan can make an incredible impression at this stage by showcasing your proactive approach and commitment to making an impact.

Companies may not always ask for a plan, but when it comes to senior or strategic roles, we actively encourage our candidates to prepare and present one. We also let the client know in advance that we'll be asking the candidate to provide one. This not only shifts how both sides approach the process—it often influences the long-term success of the role itself.

Key Points:
- A 90-day plan shows you're already thinking like someone in the role—not just a candidate.

- It demonstrates initiative, strategic thinking, and alignment with company goals.

- It offers a clear, phased approach to onboarding, learning, and delivering results.

- It helps interviewers picture your integration and contribution from day one.

A 90-day plan outlines your intended contributions and goals for your first three months on the job, divided into manageable phases. Presenting this plan demonstrates your understanding of the role and company priorities, your strategic mindset, and your dedication to driving results from day one. It also tells interviewers that you're prepared to take ownership, adapt to the company culture, and bring value immediately.

This chapter will guide you in crafting an impactful 90-day plan that's adaptable to any role. You'll learn how to structure your plan into phases, understand the key goals of each phase, and discover how to present it confidently in your interview. By the end, you'll be ready to demonstrate your vision and readiness to make a meaningful impact.

While a 90-day plan may sound like a high-level corporate tool, it's actually one of the most practical and impactful ways to show you're ready to step into a role and make a difference. If you've never created one before—don't worry. We'll walk through what it is, why it matters, and how to build one that works for you.

A 90-day plan is essentially a roadmap that outlines what you intend to achieve in your first three months in a new role. It's broken down into three phases—typically 30, 60, and 90-day segments—and focuses on how you'll learn, contribute, and make a meaningful impact. Think of it as a structured way to answer the question: *"If we hire you, what's your plan?"*

Importantly, this isn't a plan you're locked into. It's a flexible, evolving document that demonstrates foresight, initiative, and a genuine interest in aligning with the company's goals. By presenting a 90-day plan in your second interview, you're showing that you're not just there to do a job—you're there to excel in it.

Why a 90-Day Plan Matters in a Second Interview

By the time you're invited to a second interview, the hiring team already knows you have the relevant experience and skills. What they're trying to assess now is how you'll approach the role and whether you're truly ready to hit the ground running.

This is where your 90-day plan becomes your ace. It shows:

- You've done your homework and understand what's expected.

- You're a strategic thinker who doesn't wait to be told what to do.

- You care about results and are motivated to contribute from day one.

It also shows that you can work with feedback and adjust your course if needed—something every employer values.

What Is a 90-Day Plan, Really?

Let's strip it right back: a 90-day plan is a structured outline of what you'll do in your first three months in a new job.

It typically covers:

- What you'll focus on learning.

- Who you'll build relationships with.

- How you'll contribute to the team or company.

- What goals you'll aim to hit by the end of the first quarter.

You don't need to know everything about the business to draft a 90-day plan. You just need to show how you plan to integrate into the role thoughtfully and intentionally. It doesn't have to be perfect—it's a starting point, and you can (and should) position it as flexible based on what you learn in the role.

Creating a Tailored 90-Day Plan

While each role demands different priorities, the structure of a 90-day plan remains consistent. A strong 90-day plan reflects the nature of the role and the business environment you're entering. A one-size-fits-all approach doesn't cut it.

Here's how different types of roles can shape your plan:

- Sales-Focused 90-Day Plan: Prioritises lead generation, client engagement, early wins, and market research. Great for business development, account management, or revenue-focused roles.

- Operations/Management-Focused 90-Day Plan: Centres around systems, team integration, workflow optimisation, and leadership alignment.

- Universal 90-Day Plan: Perfect if you're not in a sales or leadership role. This plan blends learning, relationship-building, and early value creation, and works well for administrative, marketing, customer service, and entry-level positions.

Each plan follows the same three-phase format, allowing you to adapt it for your situation while keeping the structure clear and simple.

Breakdown of Each Phase

The First 30 Days: Orientation and Relationship-Building

Whether you're joining a startup or a global enterprise, these actions apply across the board:

- Learn the Business: Understand the products or services, company values, target market, and competitors. Read internal materials, observe meetings, and soak up as much as you can.

- Meet the People: Connect with your manager, your team, and cross-functional colleagues. These early relationships are key to feeling settled and supported.

- Master the Tools: From CRMs to project management platforms—whatever systems are used in the business, get confident with them quickly.

- Set Expectations: Align with your manager on what success looks like in this early stage. Establish 2–3 realistic, measurable goals to aim for by the end of the first month.

The Next 30 Days (Days 31–60): Deepening Knowledge and Adding Value

By now, you've got the lay of the land. This is when you shift from learning to contributing:

- Start Delivering: Step into projects or tasks that allow you to apply your strengths. Your aim here is to become someone the team can rely on.

- Ask for Feedback: Don't wait for a formal review. Proactively seek input from your manager and peers on how you're tracking.

- Spot Quick Wins: Look for inefficiencies or gaps in processes. Could something be done better? Cheaper? Faster? These insights can make a big impact.

- Build Your Internal Brand: Say yes to new opportunities. Be visible. Show your willingness to get involved and help others succeed too.

The Final 30 Days (Days 61–90): Strategy, Results, and Forward Planning

In your final stretch of the 90-day plan, it's time to show real impact and begin setting up your long-term contribution:

- Refine Your Strategy: Based on the feedback and your experience so far, adjust your approach where needed. This shows maturity and flexibility.

- Deliver Something Meaningful: Complete a task or project you can point to as a win. Even a small improvement or result can help build momentum.

- Set New Goals: Begin planning for the next 90 days. Present your goals and strategy to your manager—this shows initiative and future-focus.

- Propose Ideas: By this point, you've likely noticed areas that could benefit from innovation or improvement. Share your ideas respectfully and constructively. Even if they're not implemented immediately, it shows initiative and genuine investment.

Presenting Your Plan in an Interview

Here's the thing—anyone can draft a plan. What sets you apart is how you *present* it:

- Position it as a working draft: You're open to adapting it with feedback.

- Use clear visual structure: Whether it's a simple table, a slide, or even just a 3-phase outline, make it easy to follow.

- Speak to the company's priorities: Refer to what you've learned about the company so far—link your plan to real goals and challenges they've mentioned.

- Show enthusiasm and curiosity: This isn't a box-ticking exercise. It's your chance to express genuine excitement and drive.

The Bottom Line

Whether you're stepping into your first job, applying for a senior role, or re-entering the workforce, a 90-day plan shows that you've thought beyond the interview. You're not just interested in *getting* the job—you're already thinking about how you'll *do* the job well. Even if the interviewer never asks for a 90-day plan, having one ready gives you a huge advantage.

It makes you look prepared, mature, and ready to lead—even if you're not in a leadership role.

In ***Resources and Tools for Success*** you'll find a practical **90-day plan checklist** to help you refine your draft, prepare for your second interview, and ensure you've ticked all the right boxes.

Now that you understand the structure, purpose, and power of a well-crafted 90-day plan, you're already ahead of many candidates. You've shown initiative, foresight, and a commitment to making a meaningful impact from day one. But while the framework remains consistent, how you apply it can vary depending on the industry you're stepping into.

Every industry comes with its own language, priorities, and unspoken expectations—and recognising these nuances can take your interview performance from strong to standout. In the next chapter, we'll explore how to tailor your approach for different sectors, including tips on what hiring managers in specific industries are really looking for.

Whether you're headed into healthcare, finance, tech, education, or the creative industries, these insights will help you speak their language, anticipate their needs, and present yourself as the right person for the job—not just in theory, but in practice.

Chapter Fourteen
Tips for Specific Industries
Tailoring Your Approach Based on Industry Expectations

Not all interviews are created equal. While strong communication, preparation, and professionalism form the foundation of any great interview, the way you present yourself—and what you emphasise—should be shaped by the specific expectations of your industry. Each sector comes with its own language, norms, and non-negotiables. Some industries will expect you to have licences, clearances, or certifications ready to go. Others may care less about formal qualifications and more about your storytelling, creative process, or cultural fit.

This chapter will guide you through the practical adjustments you can make to align with industry standards, connect with your interviewers, and stand out for the right reasons.

Key Points:

- Different industries require different types of preparation, qualifications, and interview approaches.

- Licences, medical clearances, and regulatory compliance are essential in certain sectors like mining and construction.

- Project-based roles may place strong emphasis on governance, compliance, and stakeholder management.

- Understanding industry-specific systems, standards, and certifications gives you a competitive edge.

While core interview skills remain consistent, the expectations and structure of interviews in mining, healthcare, engineering, creative fields, and other sectors are shaped by unique industry requirements. In some industries, technical capabilities and regulatory knowledge are non-negotiable. In others, adaptability, communication style, or cultural fit might weigh in more.

Some industry examples:
Mining and Construction

In the mining and construction industries, interviews often involve confirming your current licences (such as white cards, high-risk work licences, or mine-site inductions), as well as your physical and mental readiness for the job. It's not uncommon to be asked about your ability to pass drug and alcohol testing, your medical fitness, and your experience working in remote or high-risk environments.

Be prepared to discuss:

- Previous FIFO (fly-in, fly-out) or DIDO (drive-in, drive-out) experience.
- Safety protocols and adherence to WHS standards.
- Exposure to specific equipment, machinery, or systems
- Work under fatigue management policies.

Bringing up your proactive attitude towards site safety or your record of zero incidents may also enhance your credibility.

Niche or Process-Specific Roles

Some businesses operate in very niche markets or offer highly specialised services. Whether it's a bespoke manufacturing process, a unique SaaS platform, or a rare compliance-based offering, these companies often look for candidates with specific system knowledge, industry exposure, or similar environment experience.

In these cases:

- Highlight similar processes, even if in different industries.

- Use terminology familiar to their space to show alignment.

- Discuss how you've adapted quickly to industry-specific systems before.

For example, if a company uses Salesforce for managing client interactions but within a unique workflow model, showing familiarity with CRM customisation or workflow integration will work in your favour.

Engineering, Architecture & Building Design

In technical professions like engineering and architecture, qualifications alone may not be enough. You may be required to hold certifications aligned with local building codes or engineering standards, especially if your previous experience is overseas.

Expect to be asked about:

- Australian Standards (AS), NCC (National Construction Code), and design regulations.

- Project lifecycle involvement – from feasibility and planning to delivery.

- Software proficiencies (AutoCAD, Revit, Inventor, etc.).

- Collaboration with contractors, clients, and councils.

Certifications such as CPEng (Chartered Professional Engineer) or RPEQ (Registered Professional Engineer of Queensland) are often essential. For international candidates, bridging qualifications or recognition through Engineers Australia may be needed.

Allied Health

In Australia, allied health roles require active registration with AHPRA (Australian Health Practitioner Regulation Agency). Without this, you are not legally permitted to practice in most roles, regardless of qualifications or overseas experience.

Common interview components include:

- Ethical scenarios testing how you manage patient rights, confidentiality, or dual relationships.

- Demonstrating your understanding of current clinical guidelines and therapy frameworks.

- Discussing multidisciplinary collaboration and your communication with GPs, families, and other healthcare providers.

- For NDIS-related roles, you may also need to show knowledge of reporting, outcome tracking, and safeguarding protocols.

Roles Emphasising Governance, Compliance, or Project Experience

In roles where governance and compliance are critical—such as in infrastructure, public sector, financial services, or healthcare operations—interviewers will be more focused around certain topics.

Common interview components include:

- Risk management frameworks.

- Project governance processes (e.g., PRINCE2, PMBOK, Agile compliance).

- Data security or legal obligations (particularly under Australian law).

- Stakeholder reporting and audit readiness.

Being able to articulate how you've worked within (or helped implement) a robust compliance framework can be a game-changer, especially in large, regulated environments.

Trades & Apprenticeships

Many candidates in trades or apprenticeship pathways may not have a polished résumé or formal interview training. However, that doesn't mean they can't make a strong impression. Interviews in this space often focus on practical reliability and trainability.

Be prepared to answer questions around:

- Time management and punctuality

- Willingness to learn and take direction

- Understanding of safety protocols (such as PPE use, site-specific rules)

- Tools and equipment experience

Some apprenticeships may also involve a basic aptitude test or practical assessment, particularly in trades like electrical, plumbing, or mechanical. These are designed to assess your comprehension, mechanical reasoning, and problem-solving abilities.

Professional Services

In professional services—such as legal, consulting, accounting, or real estate—interviews typically explore your ability to work with clients, maintain professionalism, and operate within commercial expectations.

Key areas include:

- Communication and client service

- Commercial awareness

- Ethical and regulatory compliance

- Time billing or KPI accountability

- Relevant certifications and study pertaining to the role

In professional services, interviews may also test your ability to manage deadlines, juggle multiple clients, and demonstrate commercial maturity—especially in junior roles where you'll be supporting multiple stakeholders.

International Qualifications & Industry Transitions

Transitioning industries—or countries—takes resilience. It's normal to face extra hurdles, but focusing on the skills and insights you bring makes a powerful difference. For candidates with overseas experience or those transitioning into a new industry, demonstrating relevance is key. Many professions in Australia require specific qualifications to be recognised through local authorities such as:

- Engineers Australia (for engineering qualifications)

- AHPRA (for health professionals)

- Vetassess or TRA (for trades and skilled roles)

Even if your qualifications are not yet recognised, you can still showcase transferable skills—like stakeholder management, system familiarity, or compliance exposure—that bridge the gap between your previous industry and the one you're entering.

When interviewing, ensure you highlight:

- Your adaptability and willingness to upskill.

- Any coursework, certifications, or bridging programs you've undertaken.

- Your ability to translate knowledge across contexts, especially for niche industries with similar processes or systems.

This approach not only shows preparedness but also empathy for the adjustment employers might need to make—and reassures them you're ready to hit the ground running.

Understanding the unique requirements of your industry isn't just helpful—it's expected. Demonstrating familiarity with industry standards, compliance requirements, project cycles, and client expectations positions you as a serious contender. Whether it's possessing the right certification, speaking the same technical language, or sharing real-world project examples, aligning your experience with the realities of the industry gives you a distinct edge.

When preparing, go beyond surface-level knowledge. Speak to professionals, read up on recent industry changes, and tailor your pitch to reflect both your technical abilities and your adaptability. The more nuanced your preparation, the more confident—and compelling—you'll be in any industry-specific interview.

Industry alignment doesn't end in the interview room. In a digital world, your online presence speaks volumes—often before you've even said a word. Recruiters, hiring managers, and decision-makers are increasingly turning to LinkedIn, personal websites, and even social media to get a sense of who you are beyond your résumé.

Which brings us to the next chapter—*Leveraging Social Media and Online Presence*. Your personal brand isn't just about professional polish; it's about authenticity, consistency, and telling the right story across every touchpoint. Whether you're active online or not, people are Googling you. It's time to take control of what they find—and use it to your advantage.

Chapter Fifteen
Leveraging Social Media and Online Presence
Creating a Personal Brand That Reflects Who You Are – And Owning It

When I had my second child, I returned to work just days after giving birth. It wasn't because I had something to prove — it was simply part of who I was at the time: a business owner, a mum, and someone deeply committed to both. My ex-husband, knowing how much anxiety I had about returning to work, took a photo of me in the office with our newborn in my arms. He was proud of me — and he posted it. He encouraged me to own that moment, because it represented who I was.

What followed shocked me.

The post was met with criticism. Strangers attacked my parenting, questioned the care of my children, and accused me of setting unrealistic expectations for other women. Some even suggested the photo was fake.

In hindsight, my regret wasn't posting it — it was deleting it. I let the negativity drown out the message I was trying to share: that returning to work looks different for everyone, and for me, this was part of my journey. I now speak openly about that time — about having help, about daycare, about how hard the juggle was and still is — because that's what authenticity looks like. It's not polished perfection – it's sometimes messy, always human, and very real.

Building a personal brand is more than curating the perfect image. It's about consistency in your tone, clarity in your values, and staying true to who you are — especially when it's uncomfortable. And while your personal brand lives online, the strength behind it is often built offline.

Tailored Guidance for Different Career Journeys

Students and Graduates – Start Smart

You may not have years of experience, but you *do* have something to say. Share what you're learning, what you're curious about, and what your goals are. Your LinkedIn doesn't need to look like a CEO's — it just needs to show that you're engaged, switched on, and ready to grow.

Parents Returning to Work – Reclaiming Your Voice

You are not starting from scratch — you're starting from experience. Use your online profile to reflect your strengths, your transferable skills, and your readiness. Even a small post about your return to work can help others feel less alone — and remind employers of your resilience.

Immigrants and Career Changers – Reintroducing Yourself

Whether it's a new industry or a new country, your digital presence can be your introduction. Share where you've been, where you are, and where you're going. Highlight your strengths with confidence. Your background is not a barrier — it's your point of difference.

Executives and Leaders – Lead with Purpose

People follow people, not titles. A consistent online presence reinforces your credibility and thought leadership. It also gives people a glimpse into your values and vision. You don't need to post every day — but when you do, let it be intentional.

Those Rebuilding – Rewrite the Narrative

If you've been through burnout, redundancy, or personal change, your story is still valid. A few subtle tweaks to your LinkedIn, thoughtful engagement with professional content, and a clear statement of where you're headed can speak volumes — even in silence.

For everyone – Quiet Presence, Strong Impact

Not everyone is online all the time, and that's okay. But if your profile is public, make sure it reflects you. A clean, up-to-date LinkedIn and minimal consistency across platforms is often all it takes to leave a professional impression.

Case Study: The Online Presence That Cost a Role

About eight years ago, I was representing a candidate to a new client - a Senior Marketing, Communications, and PR position based in Melbourne. On paper—and professionally—she was strong. Her LinkedIn profile was polished, thoughtful, and aligned with her industry. She had positioned herself as a thought leader, frequently sharing articles, engaging in professional conversations, and even speaking at relevant industry forums.

However, as often happens with senior or high-visibility roles, the hiring manager explored further. They viewed her public Instagram and Facebook accounts. What they found told a very different story. Weekend events, public commentary, and the tone of her posts created a disconnect. The professional brand she had so carefully curated on LinkedIn didn't match what was reflected across other platforms. It raised concerns about how she might represent the business publicly — and how she was perceived in the community. She didn't get the role.

As her recruiter, it was a turning point in how I coach candidates. Not only did it affect her candidacy — it affected my reputation. The lesson? Consistency matters. Especially in a connected world where your online presence is easily accessed and quietly assessed.

You don't need to strip back your personality or filter out your life — but you *do* need to make sure your digital brand aligns with your values and the level of role you're applying for.

Being Proactive About Your Past: Taking Ownership

It's worth noting that recruiters and hiring managers — myself included — *do* Google candidates. In fact, many companies now use scraping tools that can pull every trace of your digital footprint, including old blog posts, articles, forums, past social media profiles, and public comments. What you've said, shared, or written years ago can and often *will* resurface during the hiring process.

That's not said to scare you — it's said to empower you.

If there's something in your online history that doesn't align with who you are today, don't wait for someone else to bring it up. Take the opportunity to address it in the interview, briefly and honestly. Acknowledge it, talk about how you've grown, and where you are now. You don't need to give a speech. You just need to show that you're self-aware, accountable, and intentional in how you've evolved.

This is where authenticity truly comes into play. We've all made mistakes, posted things we outgrew, or had chapters that don't reflect our current values. What matters most is how you *own your story*, and how clearly you can demonstrate who you are now — both online and in person.

Finding the Balance Between Visibility and Professionalism

With the rise of influencers, thought leaders, and personal branding culture, it's easy to feel pressure to have a 'voice' online — to post regularly, share opinions, or open up about your life. And while there's incredible value in visibility, it also comes with responsibility. I don't claim to be an influencer or thought leader — I just know who I am, I'm connected to my purpose, and I genuinely love what I do. That's what drives how I show up online.

There's a fine balance between offering real insight and oversharing. Particularly on platforms like LinkedIn, where tone and intention can easily be misread, it's important to pause before you post and ask: *What am I really saying? How might this be perceived?*

We all bring our own context and bias to what we read online. What might feel empowering to one person could feel divisive or unprofessional to another. That doesn't mean you shouldn't speak — it means you should be intentional. Let your values guide you. Ask yourself: *If someone who doesn't know me saw this, would it reflect the brand I'm trying to build?*

Authenticity doesn't mean sharing everything. It means being real, being respectful, and being clear on the message you want to leave behind.

Tips from the Recruiter: Protecting and Projecting Your Online Brand

- **Audit your profiles regularly-** LinkedIn, Instagram, Facebook, TikTok — check them all. Look at them through the eyes of a potential employer. Would you hire you?

- **Be real, but be aligned-** Authenticity isn't about being unfiltered. It's about being clear and consistent. Let your voice be human, but aligned with how you want to be perceived.

- **Use privacy settings with intention-** If there are parts of your life you want to keep private, adjust your settings. But assume anything public may be seen.

- **Check for consistency across platforms-** Your job titles, timelines, tone, and even the content you engage with should match your career goals.

- **Act like the brand you want to work for-** The more senior the role, the more important it is to reflect the values and professionalism of the company you want to join.

Red Flags Hiring Managers Notice

- Public complaints about former employers or colleagues

- Aggressive comment threads or polarising statements

- Inconsistent job titles or dates

- Excessive filters or unprofessional photos

- Online behaviour that contradicts your stated values

Pro tip: Set a Google Alert for Your Name - It's a simple way to stay aware of how and where your name shows up online — and it gives you a chance to respond or clean up your digital footprint if needed.

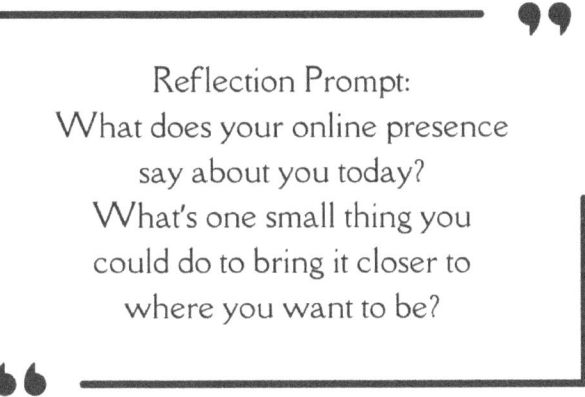

Reflection Prompt:
What does your online presence say about you today?
What's one small thing you could do to bring it closer to where you want to be?

The confidence to stand firm in your brand — especially when it's challenged — often comes from having the right people around you. I'm lucky to have a tight network: a group of strong women who've lived through the same scrutiny, male friends and mentors who uplift me, and a partner who sees me fully.

Your brand and your network are connected. One reflects who you are; the other reminds you who you are — especially when the world tries to tell you otherwise.

In the next chapter, we'll explore the power of that network. How to build it, how to nurture it, and why the people around you can be one of your greatest assets on the path to career success.

Chapter Sixteen

Networking and References

Building Genuine Connections and Leveraging Trusted Referees

There's a quiet strength in knowing who's in your corner. After facing unexpected backlash online—when all I'd done was share an honest moment about returning to work as a new mum—it was my network who held me steady. Not just publicly, but privately. They reminded me of my values, my intention, and my right to show up in the world as I am. That support didn't come from likes or followers—it came from people I trusted, who genuinely understood me and my journey. And that's the kind of network you want to build.

Networking isn't about collecting business cards or sending cold LinkedIn messages. It's about building relationships that are reciprocal, real, and rooted in respect. It's about finding those people who lift you up when you need it most—and being that person for others in return.

Throughout your career—and especially during a job search—having a trusted network can make all the difference. Whether it's a mentor who helps you prepare for an interview, a colleague who puts your name forward, or a former manager who becomes a glowing referee, your connections are part of your professional currency.

Key Points:
- Networking is about relationships, not transactions – focus on building authentic, two-way connections that lead to insight and

opportunity.

- Many jobs aren't advertised publicly – a strong network can unlock hidden roles and give you a competitive edge.

- Strong references validate your value – the right referee can reinforce your capability, professionalism, and character.

- Maintaining your network and references is a long-term game – stay in touch, offer value, and show appreciation consistently.

Shikha's Story Continued.

As mentioned earlier, Shikha applied for over 80 roles before finally landing the one that felt right. Each month, we worked together to refine her approach—focusing on visibility, confidence, and consistency. One of the biggest changes she made was using her structured résumé to build out her LinkedIn profile. A well-designed résumé becomes a valuable tool not just for job applications, but for creating your professional online presence.

I also encouraged Shikha to go beyond just applying on job boards. For every role she applied to, she searched LinkedIn to see who had posted the job—often a recruiter or hiring manager—and sent them a personalised message to introduce herself and express interest. It wasn't about pushing—it was about making a professional connection.

She also reached out to people already in roles she aspired to, including former classmates and people in similar industries. She asked them simple, strategic questions: What was the recruitment process like? Were there any opportunities coming up? Who should she speak to? These small steps created momentum. It reminded her (and me) that successful networking isn't about being the loudest person in the room—it's about being consistent, curious, and open.

Why is networking important?

Your network is made up of the people you build trust and connection with over time—not just in your current role, but across your entire career. It could include peers, mentors, former managers, clients, university contacts, training facilitators, or people you've volunteered alongside. These relationships don't just form overnight—they're built intentionally, but that doesn't mean they have to feel forced or transactional.

A trusted network offers more than job leads. It provides guidance, referrals, industry insight, and at times, emotional support. Your network can boost your visibility, open doors, and advocate for you in spaces you're not yet in. Whether you're changing industries, re-entering the workforce, starting out, or stepping up, your network grows with you—and can grow because of you.

How do I build (or rebuild) my network?

Start small. Reach out to a former colleague. Reconnect with someone you studied with. Join a professional group. You never know which message, conversation, or event might lead to your next opportunity.

Some practical ways to build or strengthen your network include:

- Attending job expos, industry panels, and local networking events

- Reaching out to former classmates, teachers, or TAFE trainers

- Following up after webinars or workshops you've attended

- Connecting with people in roles you're aspiring to

- Reaching out to mentors or leaders you admire

- Volunteering in a professional or community setting to meet like-minded people

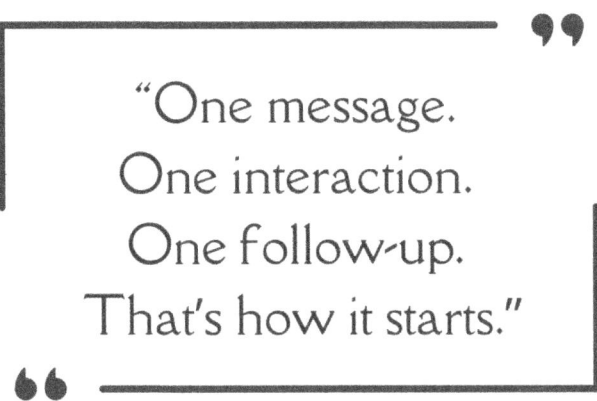

"One message.
One interaction.
One follow-up.
That's how it starts."

Using LinkedIn to connect intentionally

LinkedIn is one of the most effective tools for growing your network when used intentionally. It's not just a job board—it's a space where professionals go to share ideas, promote opportunities, and be visible.

Your profile is your digital first impression. It should reflect who you are, what you're good at, and where you're going. Use a professional photo, write a short and engaging summary, and include your experience, qualifications, and achievements—even those gained overseas or through volunteer work. This is your personal brand in action.

Once your profile is set up, start connecting—peers, mentors, recruiters, and others in your field. Engage with content. Comment thoughtfully. Share articles you've found helpful. Join industry groups and contribute to discussions. These small actions build visibility and trust over time.

Face-to-face still matters

While digital networking is incredibly powerful, don't underestimate the value of real-world interaction—especially in a world where so much of our communication happens behind screens. Meeting someone face-to-face builds trust faster, creates stronger emotional connections, and gives you the opportunity to make a memorable impression that simply can't be replicated online.

Local events, industry breakfasts, and community gatherings offer more than just networking—they give you space to practise your pitch, read body language, and connect in a way that feels human and genuine. These in-person moments often lead to deeper conversations, spontaneous opportunities, and the kind of rapport that grows into long-term professional relationships.

Before attending, prepare. Bring printed copies of your résumé – even just one or two in your bag just in case. Practise your short introduction—your elevator pitch. Research who will be there and think of a few questions to ask about their company or current hiring needs.

And don't forget to follow up. A thank-you email or a personalised LinkedIn message after the event can turn a single moment into a meaningful professional connection. Most people skip this step—but it's often the one that sets you apart. In a world where everyone is online, showing up in person—and following through—can be the thing that gets you remembered.

Asking for guidance and support

Mentors, past colleagues, teachers, and community leaders can offer valuable support—whether that's through advice, feedback, or introductions. Most people are happy to help when asked respectfully and clearly.

Be specific when you reach out. Let them know what you're working on, what kind of support you're looking for, and why you value their perspective. It's not about asking for a job—it's about asking for insight, encouragement, or direction.

Examples of what to say

Sometimes the hardest part is knowing how to start. Here are a few message templates to get you going:

- **LinkedIn connection request** - *Hi [Name], I came across your profile and was really impressed by your work in [industry/company]. I'm currently exploring similar opportunities and would love to connect. Thanks so much.*

- **Requesting a mentor** - *Dear [Name], I recently saw your [post/presentation/work] and found it incredibly valuable. I'm early in my career and would be grateful for the chance to learn from you. Would you be open to a short conversation?*

- **Reaching out to a recruiter or hiring manager** - *Subject: Interest in [Job Title] Role at [Company Name] Dear [Hiring Manager's Name], I hope you're well. I'm writing regarding the [Job Title] role you've advertised. With experience in [key area], I believe I can add value to your team. I'd love the opportunity to connect and learn more. I'm available [insert times] and look forward to hearing from you.*

Referees: Your voice when you're not in the room

Referees are more than a formality—they're the final voice that supports your application. A great referee confirms your strengths, attitude, and contribution in a way that helps employers feel confident saying yes.

But don't leave references to the last minute. Manage them with the same care and professionalism you'd give the rest of your application.

Tips for managing references:

- Always ask permission before listing someone

- Never assume they're comfortable or available to speak

- Let them know what role you're applying for and what you'd appreciate them highlighting

- Keep them updated on your progress

- Follow up with a genuine thank you

Some larger companies have strict HR policies that limit what a referee can say—they might only confirm your employment dates and job title. In these cases, consider asking someone else in the business who worked closely with you, or someone who has since moved on and is comfortable speaking more freely. Sometimes referees will say no. It could be due to policy, discomfort, or a breakdown in the relationship. That's why staying in touch—and leaving well—matters.

Finding the right referee for your situation

No matter where you are in your career, there's always someone who can speak to your value. If you're a school leaver, ask a teacher, coach, or career advisor. If you're studying at TAFE, consider a trainer or placement supervisor. If you're re-entering the workforce, references from voluntary work are not only valid—they're powerful. They reflect initiative, reliability, and community spirit. If you're in a leadership or sales role, client references are often incredibly valuable. They show how you build relationships, deliver outcomes, and maintain integrity. Mentors or people you've mentored can also be excellent referees—they offer insight into how you show up for others, not just yourself.

References don't need to be formal to be meaningful—they just need to be genuine, relevant, and reflective of who you are.

Networking is Not Just a Tool – It's a Lifeline

Networking and references aren't just tools—they're relationships. Over the past five years, through my work with Headspace and Queensland Government's Mentoring for Growth program, I've met hundreds of candidates, small business owners, and not-for-profit leaders. In almost every conversation, the same truth comes up: a trusted network is a powerful career and business asset. It's not about how many people you know—it's about the handful of people you truly align with. When you invest in their vision, grow with them, and genuinely support one another, you create a ripple effect that leads to confidence, connection, and opportunities you never saw coming.

At a recent speaking event hosted by the Volunteering Collective and City of Gold Coast, I met incredible individuals like the inspirational Ian Grace, the founders of *Serve the City*, a Brisbane and Gold Coast-based NFP, and Wayne, the President from *Cycling Without Age*.

Cycling Without Age is a global movement with a beautiful mission—offering free trishaw rides to seniors and people with limited mobility, helping them reconnect with their communities and the joy of being outdoors. On the Gold Coast, the program has been embraced by local volunteers and aged care facilities alike, bringing smiles, stories, and a sense of freedom to those who often feel forgotten.

Wayne later joined the Mentoring for Growth program as a mentee, and through our connection, I introduced him to others in my network. What came next wasn't just professional growth—it was a sense of support and belief. It gave him the space to be vulnerable, to find confidence, and to realise he was on the right path. That's the real power of a strong network. Whether you're a candidate or a small business owner, it starts with asking questions, being open, and aligning with the right people. Those few genuine relationships—your champions—will walk beside you as you grow.

> Mentor Moment: Why I Love Networking
>
> "Helping small businesses grow through my network is something I'm deeply committed to—because I wish I had that support 10 years ago. Now, when I meet someone with purpose and drive, I want to share that network and walk alongside them. Sometimes all it takes is five or six people who believe in you. They become your champions."

They're not just tools – they're extensions of your professional brand. They reflect how you show up, how you treat people, and how you build trust over time. Whether you're just entering the workforce, navigating a career change, or stepping into leadership, the relationships you form—and how you nurture them—will often open more doors than any application ever could. These connections are built through consistency, strengthened through shared values, and maintained through mutual respect.

By now, you've taken meaningful steps toward building your professional presence—establishing a strong network, learning how to ask for support, and choosing referees who will advocate for you with confidence. You've done the work to position yourself clearly, to grow connections that matter, and to be seen.

Now comes the part many people dread but absolutely need to embrace: *negotiating your worth*. Whether you're going for your first role or your next leadership step, knowing how to discuss salary with clarity, professionalism, and self-assurance is key to progressing in your career. In the next chapter, we'll explore how to approach salary conversations without fear—covering research, timing, tone, and how to respond to offers in a way that reflects your value.

You've earned your seat at the table. Now let's make sure it comes with the package you deserve.

Chapter Seventeen

Salary Negotiation Strategies

Confidently Navigating the Conversation to Secure What You're Worth

It can feel intimidating and even uncomfortable, but it is an essential step in securing a role that reflects your value. While candidates often focus on their worth, employers look at a range of factors, including the market, the demands of the role, and the overall onboarding process. Striking a balance between your expectations and the employer's perspective is key to successful negotiation.

A Note About Recruiters and Salary Representation
If you're applying for roles through a recruiter, it's important to understand how they're compensated. Most recruitment agencies are paid a percentage of the candidate's total salary package—meaning the higher your salary, the higher their commission. While many recruiters advocate ethically and transparently on your behalf, there are some who may inflate your salary expectations without your knowledge.

This might mean quoting the employer a figure above what you've actually agreed to or what you feel comfortable with. The risk? It can price you out of the role entirely, especially if the company is working within a strict budget. Worse still, you may be asked about your salary expectations directly in the interview—only to be blindsided by the difference between what the recruiter has quoted and what you're prepared to accept.

This kind of misrepresentation doesn't just damage trust—it can make you appear inconsistent or unprofessional when you've done nothing wrong. If you're working with a recruiter, ask them to confirm in writing what salary they've put forward to the client. Transparency is key. You deserve to know how you're being represented and to have full control over how your expectations are communicated.

Key Points:
For Candidates:

- Ground your salary expectations in research and market realities.

- Focus on the value you bring, not just your personal circumstances.

- Be flexible and open to alternative forms of compensation, including review clauses.

For Employers:

- Define salary bands early and factor in onboarding costs.

- Be transparent and consistent during negotiations.

- Use review clauses to balance initial salary offers with long-term value.

Understanding the Context

When approaching salary discussions, it's important to recognise that every role and organisation is different. Some roles come with clearly defined salary bands, while others are more flexible, with employers waiting to assess the value a candidate brings. Regardless of the scenario, preparation is critical. Use the following steps to set yourself up for a productive discussion:

Do Your Research

Investigate market trends, industry benchmarks, and salary ranges for similar roles in your location (or even other states). Use tools like salary surveys, networking, and job boards to ensure your expectations are grounded in reality—because going in too high or too low can impact how you're perceived and the strength of your negotiation.

Evaluate Your Value

Consider your skills, experience, and achievements compared to the requirements of the role. Be honest about what you bring to the table, but also realistic—if you're transitioning from another industry or have limited direct experience, factor in the time it may take to get up to speed and demonstrate your full value.

Be Realistic About Onboarding

Employers invest time and resources in onboarding. Even if you're confident in your abilities, there will be an adjustment period as you learn the systems, processes, and culture of the organisation. This is especially important when negotiating for higher pay—your value will need to justify the investment from day one.

Understanding Your Work Rights in Australia

If you're new to the Australian job market—whether you're a recent graduate, someone re-entering the workforce, or a newly arrived immigrant—salary negotiation can feel daunting. You might be unsure what's fair, what's legal, or how to respond when offered a role. One of the most powerful ways to prepare is by understanding your rights as a worker in Australia.

Australia has strong workplace laws designed to ensure employees are treated fairly and respectfully. These protections are part of a national framework that sets clear standards for pay, working conditions, and employer obligations. Whether you're applying for your first job or stepping into a more senior role, knowing the basics gives you the confidence to advocate for yourself.

Here are a few key work rights all employees in Australia should be aware of:

- **Minimum Wage** – Australia sets a national minimum wage that is reviewed annually by the Fair Work Commission. This wage is the legal minimum any employer must pay based on a 38-hour work week.

- **No Unpaid Work** – All work must be paid unless it falls under an approved, lawful unpaid arrangement (e.g. formal internships or recognised volunteer roles).

- **Superannuation Contributions** – Employers must contribute to your superannuation regardless of how much you earn or how many hours you work.

- **National Employment Standards (NES)** – These are 11 minimum entitlements that apply to all employees, including leave, hours of work, and termination notice.

- **Award and Enterprise Agreement Pay Rates** – Some roles have specific pay rates and conditions that exceed the minimum wage. Be sure you know which award or agreement applies to you.

For job seekers unfamiliar with local standards, being informed is empowering. It not only helps you negotiate more confidently, but also ensures you're protected from unfair treatment. Understanding your rights isn't confrontational—it's preparation.

The Right Time to Talk About Salary

Discussing salary during an interview can feel like walking a tightrope—it's crucial but must be approached tactfully. One of the biggest mistakes candidates make is bringing up salary too early or doing so in a way that feels transactional. As a recruiter with years of experience, I've seen how this can leave a poor impression, especially when candidates seem more interested in the paycheck than the role itself.

Avoid the Upfront Salary Trap

When you're going through a recruiter, there's often a buffer provided by the recruiter handling the initial salary discussions. This can shield you from making a misstep, as the recruiter sets expectations on both sides. However, not every candidate is lucky enough to have this support, and even some recruiters may not fully prepare you for this conversation. If you're on your own, gauge the room and wait for the appropriate moment to raise salary-related questions—usually when the interviewer opens the door by discussing compensation or expectations.

In sales-focused roles especially, I've noticed candidates can sometimes be overly forthright about salary—some even to the point of making demands early in the interview process. Statements like "I wouldn't proceed unless the salary is above X amount" not only put off hiring managers but can also undermine your credibility. Employers want to feel that you're invested in the role and the company, not just the money.

Do Your Research

Before stepping into any interview, make sure you've researched the salary band for the role. Sites like Seek, Glassdoor, or even the job posting itself often include salary information, so there's no excuse to be blindsided. If you're aiming higher than the advertised band, ensure you've got the credentials and examples to back it up. Use your experience, projects, and measurable achievements to showcase why you're worth more. But, remember, salary discussions are better framed as a collaborative conversation, not a negotiation battle.

When to Bring it Up

If salary hasn't been addressed by the end of the interview, it's perfectly fine to ask if there's an opportunity to discuss compensation and expectations. A polite way to approach this might be, "I'd like to better understand how the compensation aligns with the expectations for the role. Is now a good time to have that discussion?" This phrasing shows that you're thoughtful, professional, and tactful.

By waiting for the right time and positioning the conversation appropriately, you'll avoid the risk of seeming overly focused on money, which can detract from your overall candidacy. Remember, salary discussions should feel like a natural progression of the interview—not the starting point.

A Recruiter's Perspective

As a recruiter, I often act as a bridge between candidates and clients. My role is to manage expectations on both sides, ensuring alignment and fostering productive conversations. A memorable instance during the COVID-19 pandemic serves as a clear example of how complex salary discussions can be, especially when the market and workplace expectations are shifting.

When offices began reopening after extended periods of remote work, I had a candidate approach me, stating they deserved $20,000 more simply because they were now expected to commute to the office. Interestingly, this was how they initiated the conversation—before we even delved into their experience, skill set, or reasons for leaving their current role. Their frustration was palpable, rooted in the inconvenience of transitioning back to in-person work after a prolonged period of working from home. They expressed dissatisfaction with the fact that many roles at the time were requiring employees to return to the office, which they felt no longer aligned with their lifestyle or preferences.

While I empathised with their perspective—acknowledging the rising cost of living, commuting expenses, and the shift in work-life balance expectations—I also recognised that this reasoning alone might not resonate with potential employers. I posed a question to encourage deeper reflection:

"What else are you bringing to the table that sets you apart from other candidates? What makes you worth $20,000 more outside of the requirement to travel?"

Their response revealed a lack of consideration for their broader value. They reiterated that the additional $20,000 was simply because they would need to commute and mentioned that other roles offered similar pay with the benefit of remaining remote. It became clear that they were approaching the negotiation from a place of personal convenience rather than focusing on how their skills, experience, or unique contributions justified their salary expectations.

I wished them well in their job search and offered a few suggestions for finding fully remote roles, pointing them toward specific strategies to better identify opportunities that aligned with their needs. I also encouraged them to think critically about their experience, how they could position themselves as a stronger candidate, and what steps they might take to expand their skill set in the meantime.

This interaction highlighted a fundamental truth about salary negotiations: expectations must be tied to the value a candidate brings to the role, not just external factors like commuting or lifestyle preferences.

Employers hire based on what a candidate can deliver, not solely on the conditions of employment. While personal factors like travel costs or convenience may be valid considerations for a candidate, they don't automatically justify a higher salary unless accompanied by a clear demonstration of skills, experience, and potential impact.

Moreover, this scenario reinforced the importance of attention to detail in the hiring process. The job advertisement for this role had explicitly stated that it required full-time, in-office work. Overlooking this critical detail raised a red flag for me as a recruiter.

Attention to detail isn't just about catching obvious errors; it reflects how a candidate approaches tasks, processes information, and considers all relevant factors in their decision-making. These are qualities employers value highly, especially in roles where precision and accountability are essential.

Ultimately, the conversation served as a reminder that candidates must approach negotiations with preparation, clarity, and a focus on what they bring to the table. While external factors are important to acknowledge, the core of any salary discussion should revolve around demonstrable value and alignment with the role's requirements.

For employers, this underscores the need for transparency in job advertisements and the importance of evaluating not just a candidate's qualifications, but their ability to approach the process with professionalism and an understanding of the bigger picture.

Position Yourself as the Best Candidate

Employers often compare multiple candidates during the hiring process. It's crucial to focus on what sets you apart, such as:

- Specific achievements in previous roles

- Unique skills or certifications relevant to the position

- Your ability to hit the ground running and deliver results

Confidence in your abilities is important, but it must be balanced with humility and an awareness of the employer's perspective.

Overconfidence can come across as arrogance, particularly when it's not backed by evidence. For instance, expecting a higher salary purely due to commuting requirements or personal circumstances may appear out of touch with the role's expectations. Instead, frame your request around the value you bring and how you can positively impact the organisation.

Be Flexible and Open-Minded

Salary isn't the only component of a compensation package. Consider benefits such as:
- Flexible working arrangements
- Bonuses or incentives tied to performance
- Professional development opportunities

If the employer can't meet your salary expectations, these additional benefits may make up the difference.

Ask the Right Questions

During the hiring process, it's okay to seek clarity. Some examples include:
- "What salary range has been allocated for this position?"
- "How does my experience compare to other candidates you're considering?"
- "Are there additional benefits or incentives tied to this role?"

These questions show that you're engaged and focused on aligning your expectations with the employer's priorities.

Using Review Periods as a Negotiation Strategy

If a salary offer is lower than expected, proposing a review period can be an effective way to find common ground. This strategy involves agreeing to a salary review at the three- or six-month mark, often aligned with the end of the probation period.

Why This Works

For Candidates: It provides an opportunity to prove your value and secure a higher salary once you've demonstrated your capabilities.

For Employers: It reduces the risk of overpaying initially and allows time to assess the candidate's contributions.

How to Implement It

- Propose a Formal Review: Suggest that your performance and contributions be evaluated at a set time, with the possibility of a salary adjustment based on achieving agreed-upon goals.

- Define Clear Goals: Work with the employer to establish measurable targets for success during the review period.

- Document the Agreement: Ensure this review clause is included in your employment contract to provide clarity and accountability.

Building Trust During the Review Period

The probation period is about more than just meeting expectations. It's an opportunity to build trust and demonstrate your value. During this time:

- Focus on Delivering Results: Track your achievements and ensure you're meeting the goals set by the employer.

- Communicate Regularly: Keep your manager updated on your

progress and seek feedback.

- Prepare for the Review Discussion: Use the review as an opportunity to showcase your contributions and renegotiate your salary.

Compensation Beyond Base Salary

When negotiating your salary, it's important to think about the total compensation package rather than just the base salary. Many roles, particularly in management or sales, include additional benefits and incentives that can significantly impact your overall earnings and job satisfaction. Some key elements to consider include:

Commission and Incentive Structures

If your role is tied to the company's revenue or profit, it's common for employers to offer:

- Short-Term Incentives (STIs): Bonuses linked to immediate or quarterly outcomes, such as achieving sales targets or project milestones.

- Long-Term Incentives (LTIs): Bonuses tied to broader, long-term objectives, such as company growth or share performance over several years.

When discussing these incentives:

- Ask about the frequency and timing of payments (e.g., monthly, quarterly, annually).

- Clarify how achievable these targets are to understand how realistic it is to earn the full incentive.

- Request information on past performance payouts to gauge consistency.

Car Allowances and Vehicle Use

For roles requiring regular travel, such as sales or account management, a car allowance or company-provided vehicle may be part of your package. In Australia, car allowances typically range from $15,000 to $20,000 on top of your base salary if a vehicle isn't provided.

When negotiating, ask:

- Whether the allowance is part of your total salary package or an additional benefit.

- How travel expectations align with the provided allowance or vehicle.

Flexibility and Well-Being Benefits

Beyond monetary compensation, many companies offer non-monetary benefits to enhance job satisfaction, such as:

- Flexible Working Arrangements: Options like work-from-home, compressed workweeks (e.g., nine-day fortnights), or hybrid models.

- Well-Being Benefits: Wellness programs, gym memberships, or mental health support.

These perks can be valuable, particularly if work-life balance is a priority for you. When evaluating an offer, consider how these benefits complement the base salary and how they align with your personal and professional needs.

Advice for Employers

From an employer's perspective, salary negotiations require balancing a candidate's expectations with the budget and the value they bring. Some key considerations include:

- Establish Clear Salary Bands: Define a range based on market trends and the role's requirements before starting the hiring process. Be prepared to justify your offer with concrete data.

- Factor in Onboarding Costs: Recognise that new hires require time and resources to get up to speed. Ensure your offer reflects both the candidate's potential and the investment you'll make during the onboarding period.

- Consider Review Clauses: Including a probationary review period can attract high-quality candidates and ensure alignment with performance expectations.

Salary negotiation is a two-way street that requires preparation, communication, and a willingness to compromise. By approaching the process with confidence and professionalism, you can ensure a positive outcome for both yourself and the organisation.

For new job seekers, those returning to work, or candidates unfamiliar with the local job market, understanding your rights and preparing ahead of time is essential. Being informed puts you in the best possible position—not only to advocate for fair pay but to begin your next role with confidence, clarity, and the respect you deserve.

Remember, negotiation isn't about being aggressive or demanding—it's about knowing your value, asking the right questions, and having an open conversation about expectations. The goal is to find alignment: a balance between what the company needs and what you bring to the table. That mindset not only sets you up for success—it also sets the tone for your working relationship from day one.

And once the negotiation is complete and the interview wraps up, your job isn't quite finished. What you do next—how you follow up—can either strengthen or weaken the impression you've made. A thoughtful, well-timed follow-up shows that you're proactive, engaged, and genuinely invested in the opportunity. It's a simple step that's often overlooked, but it can make all the difference.

Chapter Eighteen
Follow-Up After the Interview
Closing the Loop – Leave a Lasting Impression With the Right Follow-Up

The moments after an interview can be just as important as the ones spent in the room. While preparation, presence, and performance help you stand out during the interview itself, what you do afterwards plays a defining role in how you're remembered—and whether you're invited back. Follow-up is more than just good etiquette; it's your opportunity to reinforce your value, maintain momentum, and show that you're genuinely invested in the process.

Whether you're applying for a role, progressing to a second interview, or staying in touch for future opportunities, how and when you follow up matters. In today's competitive job market, the candidates who take this stage seriously are often the ones who leave the strongest impression.

Why Follow-Up Matters

Following up is a clear reflection of your professional standards. It signals that you respect the interviewer's time, that you're engaged in the process, and that you're thinking one step ahead. It's also a moment to demonstrate your communication style, reliability, and emotional intelligence—traits that don't always show up on a résumé but make a lasting impact.

Employers pay close attention to how candidates follow through. A timely, thoughtful follow-up shows commitment and maturity. It allows you to reinforce the connection you've made, clarify anything that wasn't fully covered, and guide the next steps with purpose. On the flip side, silence can leave a gap—and in some cases, cause doubt about your interest or attention to detail.

Done well, your follow-up gives you an edge. Especially when multiple candidates perform well in interviews, that simple gesture of a clear and considered message can be the tie-breaker. It's your chance to remind them why you're not just capable—but ready.

Timing, Tone, and Tools

When it comes to following up, the 'when' and the 'how' are just as important as the 'what'. Ideally, you want to send your follow-up message within 24 hours of the interview. The conversation will still be fresh in everyone's mind, and your promptness shows you're organised and engaged. Wait too long, and you risk missing that window of momentum.

Email is the most common and appropriate format for professional follow-up. Keep it clean, clear, and direct. Text messages should only be used if that was the employer's preferred communication method throughout the process. Phone calls are rarely necessary unless specifically invited or unless you've built a deeper rapport.

Match your tone to the formality of the interview. A relaxed phone screen might call for a warm and conversational tone, whereas a panel interview for an executive role calls for polish and precision. Either way, clarity and authenticity always matter.

What to Include in a Follow-Up Email

Your message doesn't need to be long—but it does need to be intentional. Open with a sincere thank you. Acknowledge the time the interviewer gave you and mention anything specific you appreciated about the conversation. Then reaffirm your interest in the role, tying it back to a strength or insight you shared. You can also use this space to clarify or expand on a point you touched on in the interview, or to reinforce how your values align with the company's.

If you're excited to move forward, say so. If you're not, that's okay too—but it's important to close the loop respectfully. Employers remember candidates who communicate with clarity and care.

End your email by confirming next steps (if they were discussed), or by expressing that you're looking forward to hearing from them once they've progressed their process. Keep it professional, but also human. This is about connection, not just protocol.

Following Up When You Know There's a Next Step

If you've been told there's a second interview or task coming up, use your follow-up as a way to show you're already thinking ahead. Reconfirm any agreed timelines or deliverables, express your enthusiasm, and briefly acknowledge what's coming next—whether it's preparing a case study, completing an assessment, or meeting the broader team.

This approach positions you as proactive, reliable, and switched-on. It also gives the employer confidence that you're ready to step into the next phase with focus and follow-through.

When You Haven't Heard Back

Sometimes, hiring timelines shift or stall—and silence from the employer can be unsettling. If a week or more has passed with no update, a polite check-in is entirely appropriate. Keep it professional and relaxed. Acknowledge that things may still be moving behind the scenes, and reiterate your interest while asking if there's any update available.

Avoid sounding impatient or frustrated. You don't know what's happening internally, and your grace in the face of uncertainty speaks volumes about how you handle ambiguity—something highly valued in many workplaces.

And if the outcome isn't in your favour? Still follow up. A brief note to thank them for the opportunity and to wish them well leaves a lasting, positive impression. It also keeps the door open for future roles—because being remembered well is always a good thing.

If You Decide Not to Proceed

You might walk out of an interview and realise the role isn't the right fit—and that's perfectly okay. What matters is how you communicate that decision. Declining an offer or choosing not to progress should still be handled with gratitude and professionalism.

Thank the interviewer for their time and for the chance to learn more about the role. Be honest (but kind) about your decision, and leave things on a positive note. You never know when your paths might cross again—or who they might refer you to.

Tailoring Your Message Based on the Process

As we explored in earlier chapters—particularly Chapters Two, Three, and Nine—a strong follow-up message only works when built on a strong foundation. If you've asked great questions, paid attention to the company's goals, and read the room well during the interview, you'll have more than enough insights to create a follow-up that's meaningful—not generic.

Who you're following up with also plays a role. A thank you to a recruiter may lean towards confirming next steps, while a note to a hiring manager or business owner might reiterate your alignment with their vision or values. Every message should feel personal and relevant.

It also matters where you are in the process. If it's early days, focus on enthusiasm and fit. If it's a final round or a meeting with a senior leader, your message should reflect that weight—highlighting your readiness and appreciation.

Pro Tips for Polished Follow-Up

- **Personalise everything**
  Avoid copying and pasting a template. Mention something specific from the interview to show you were present, engaged, and genuinely interested.

- **Proof it before you hit send**
  Spelling, grammar and tone still count—even in a quick email. A small error can dilute a strong impression.

- **Keep it brief but meaningful**
  Three to five lines is often enough. Respect your reader's time,

and let your clarity speak for itself.

- **Don't chase too soon**
  If you've already followed up once, give it a week before checking in again. Patience is part of professionalism.

- **Use a clear subject line**
  Examples include:
  Thank You – [Your Name], Interview for [Job Title]
  Following Up – [Your Name], Interview on [Date]

- **Express interest — or exit gracefully**
  Whether you're keen to continue or have chosen to step away, always communicate clearly. Your integrity matters.

- **Use templates wisely**
  Templates are a helpful starting point, but they should never replace intention. Edit them to reflect your voice, the role, and the person you're writing to.

- **Send it within 24 hours**
  That window of time post-interview is your best opportunity to stay top of mind and keep momentum.

Your follow-up is the final chapter in your interview story—so don't leave it blank. Whether you're confirming next steps, showing your appreciation, or stepping away from the process, how you handle this moment will shape how you're remembered. It's not just what you say, it's *how* you say it—and *when*.

Even if the role doesn't work out, the way you close the loop reflects maturity, confidence, and professionalism. That email may be remembered down the track. It may be forwarded to someone else. Or it may simply reinforce that you're the kind of person people want on their team.

If you're unsure how to begin or want a base to work from, I've included templates in the **Resources and Tools for Success** section to help you tailor your follow-up with clarity and confidence.

As we move into the final chapter, *Final Thoughts*, we'll explore how technology, recruiters, and your own growth mindset all play a role in shaping your career journey.

Because interviews are only one part of the story. What you do before, during *and* after will set you apart—and your growth doesn't stop here.

Chapter Nineteen

Shikha's Story

From Quiet Beginnings to Senior Technician

Shikha's journey is one of persistence, self-belief, and quiet power.

We worked together for over eight months—countless hours of coaching, deep strategy sessions, honest conversations, and more than 150 emails.

Shikha showed up every single time. Whether it was rewriting her résumé, prepping for an interview, or recovering from a setback, she did the work—graciously and consistently.

The opportunity that changed everything came through another recruiter. A casual role, barely advertised, no interview preparation, no support. On paper, it looked like a throwaway. But Shikha treated it like gold.

After THE interview, she sent me this message:

"Hi Tanya, My interview just finished. I think it went pretty well. They seemed to like me. I asked them if there was any reason that I wouldn't get the job. They said that they were looking for someone with a science background and that it is good that I am willing to learn as well. I'm just waiting to hear back from them."

– *Shikha, 12 June 2024*

I replied straight away: "Yay!! Am I reference?"

She responded: "They didn't ask for any, but if they do, I can put your details in."

A few days later:

"Hi Tanya, I've been asked to provide two referees for them to contact. What referees do you think I should send them?" – *Shikha, 20 June 2024*

We confirmed her choices together. I was proud to be one of them. And then, on 24 June, my phone rang. Shikha called to tell me she got the job! Quiet, calm, and full of happy confidence. *Me? I was bouncing out of my chair with excitement.*

I checked in the next day, and she followed up with: "Hi Tanya, Sorry I couldn't get back to you. I will be starting on Monday, 1st July." – *Shikha, 30 June 2024*

When I asked how she felt, she said: "Yeah! I'm excited, a little nervous but mostly excited!"

Her story has been one of the biggest highlights of my professional career.

That role, which started as a casual opportunity with little fanfare, ended up changing everything. There was no prep from the recruiter, barely a job description, and no expectations set—just a date, a time, and a location. But Shikha showed up anyway. She brought curiosity, quiet confidence, and a willingness to learn—despite the uncertainty.

And Shikha? She's now a Senior Technician—in a workplace where she feels mentored, supported, and genuinely valued. Her story is proof that sometimes it's not about having all the answers or a perfect plan—it's about showing up, saying yes, and letting your work speak for you. The right opportunity doesn't always look perfect on paper—but the right mindset can turn it into something extraordinary.

She didn't just get the job—she grew into it, and then beyond it.

We recently reconnected after a little while—still staying in touch, of course—but it was time for a proper catch-up. I reminded her to update her LinkedIn profile, keep a record of all the incredible work she's doing, and continue setting herself up for future opportunities—whether it's a promotion, an internal move, or a whole new path.

And hearing how well she's doing now… it honestly lifted me. Watching her growth from mentee to confident professional has been one of the most rewarding parts of what I do. We've got a long-overdue coffee catch-up to book—but for now, I'm just so proud of how far she's come.

Her story is a reminder that your breakthrough might not come with fireworks. It might start with a quiet opportunity, a moment of doubt, or a role others overlook. But if you show up, do the work, and back yourself… incredible things can happen.

Shikha didn't wait for the perfect moment—she created it.

And you can too.

Chapter Twenty

Final Thoughts

AI, the Role of Recruiters, and Your Own Continuous Improvement

As we wrap up this journey, I want to challenge some of the myths about hiring, remind you what really matters, and help you align with the kind of work that brings out your best. This chapter isn't about final words—it's about new beginnings.

Tan Rant: The Myth of the "Efficient" Hire

I often get asked if recruiters will become extinct due to the increasing use of AI in the hiring process. The short answer is no. The long answer? What kind of company wouldn't bother to read every résumé and cover letter when going through job applications? Sadly, many do, using AI or CTRL+F to match candidates' keywords with the job brief. It's a well-known practice among both internal and external recruiters. So now, as a candidate, having accepted this, how would I feel about not even meeting or speaking with someone when asked to answer interview questions? Or being required to send a video about myself for a faceless person to judge my worth?

Job seekers, whether they're desperate for a new role, eager to leave their current one, or aiming to move up, deserve more than automation. They don't care if you, the hiring manager, are trying to be more efficient. They want to connect with someone, get feedback, and understand the role and company better. People trust and work with people, and your hiring process shapes their first impression, onboarding experience, and potential employment journey.

Managers, think about it—during the probationary period, you may find you have an issue with a team member. How did you engage with them initially? How consistent have you been? And put yourself in their shoes: how would you feel if your first interaction with the company wasn't even with a real person?

So the longer answer here is no, provided companies are genuinely investing in their people.

They won't lean too heavily on AI if they want to attract individuals who align with their culture and purpose, are engaged, and will contribute to their overall success.

While AI can shorten vetting times and create efficiencies, the effort you put into a hire is directly proportionate to what you get out of a hire. If you're left wondering why your fantastic talent acquisition poses a misfit with culture or a disconnect, perhaps a ten-minute phone call to a potential applicant or more time spent in the beginning reaps benefits in the future.

Job hunting, applying, interviewing, and waiting for feedback is not just tedious; it can be exhausting and, more often than not, a blow to one's confidence. There's a perception that hiring has evolved—thanks to all the processes and automation introduced over the last 15 years. But, in reality, we haven't changed much about the way we interview. If anything, we've stayed the same or even regressed. There's often little regard for the candidate's stage in life, the experiences they bring, or what they're genuinely seeking. Companies are also overlooking how current or future life circumstances might impact someone's progress, missing the opportunity to ask what support might be needed and to show flexibility to work with them through life's ups and downs. How many good people have they missed?

Automated processes, while efficient, can feel impersonal. It often comes down to the bottom line—efficiency and fitting people into roles to get the job done. It's about increasing profit, but ironically, it's rarely about real growth or evolution.

I constantly see posts on social media or LinkedIn from companies that proudly display their 'Employer of the Year' awards, and, ironically, they seem to genuinely believe they deserve it. Having worked with some of these companies or interviewed multiple people from them, I know these awards are often won by highlighting key strengths, crafting responses that fit the award criteria perfectly, and generating votes through advertising.

Retention always starts with how you interview. Job satisfaction isn't just about support and progression—it's also about consistency and genuine consideration.

Unlocking Your State of Flow in Your Career

So if it's not just about process, what is it really about? It's about connection. About knowing where you thrive and being intentional about your next move. One of the most transformative ways to gain clarity about your career is to reflect on the moments when everything just clicked. This feeling—often described as being in a state of flow—occurs when work feels effortless, you're highly productive, and you're fully immersed in the task at hand.

When coaching candidates, I often ask them to think back to a time when they were in a role—whether it was their most recent job, their very first one, or even a position they took on unexpectedly. I encourage them to consider what kind of projects they were working on, what team they were a part of, and what was happening on that particular day or during that specific period that made work feel easy and fulfilling. The answers to these questions often hold the key to understanding the type of work that brings someone the most satisfaction.

A Real-Life Example: Emma's Journey

Take Emma, for instance. She was in the midst of exploring a career move and initially focused on industry, leadership opportunities, and her ability to build teams. On paper, she was searching for a role that aligned with her experience in leading teams, shaping company direction, and driving business growth.

However, when we shifted the conversation to her state of flow, an entirely new perspective emerged. Rather than being solely motivated by leadership and team-building, Emma realised she thrived on creating something from the ground up. Her true passion lay in taking an idea and developing a structured plan, testing it in the market and refining it based on feedback, engaging with both internal and external stakeholders to align objectives, and seeing the project through from ideation to full implementation.

By stepping back and analysing these moments, we uncovered a pattern—Emma's most fulfilling work had been in start-ups and scale-ups. While she initially thought she should remain in the tech space, it became clear that her real strength was in operational execution. Emma was at her best when working in companies that had outgrown their start-up phase but still required structure, strategy, and processes to drive them toward their next level of growth. This shift in perspective changed everything about how she approached her job search.

The Role of Flow in Career Decisions

This is a pattern I see frequently among Operations Managers, General Managers, and Senior Leaders. Many professionals assume their next role should be a direct extension of their past experience, but the real question should be: what type of work puts you in a state of flow?

For some, it's the thrill of sales and negotiation. For others, it's problem-solving and strategising. Some find their flow in mentoring teams and building relationships, while others experience it in hands-on, high-stakes execution.

When considering your next career move, take a moment to reflect on when you've felt truly engaged and energised at work. What tasks felt effortless and fulfilling? What kind of environment or role allowed you to do your best work? Were you leading, creating, strategising, problem-solving, or executing?

Recognising these patterns can help you identify roles that align with your strengths and natural flow, leading to greater job satisfaction, success, and career fulfilment.

How to Find Your State of Flow

If you're unsure how to pinpoint your moments of flow, try this. Think about a time when you loved what you were doing. It doesn't have to be a job title—it could be a specific project, task, or even a workday that felt seamless. Identify the common elements. What was the work environment like? Were you working independently or in a team? What were the challenges that excited you? Consider how you can replicate that in your next role. If you thrived in a high-growth company, would you enjoy another fast-paced environment? If you loved creative problem-solving, would a role in strategy or consulting be fulfilling?

These insights will serve as a career compass, guiding you toward opportunities that allow you to operate at your peak performance.

Your Flow State and Interviewing

Understanding your state of flow can also transform the way you approach job interviews. When asked about past achievements, you can tie them directly to the moments where you felt most engaged. Instead of simply listing job duties, focus on the work that energised you and played to your strengths.

For example, instead of saying: "In my last role, I managed a team of 10 and oversaw operations," you could say: "I thrive in environments where I can take an early-stage business and implement structure, strategy, and systems. My last role allowed me to do exactly that—leading a team of 10, I built a scalable operations process that increased efficiency by 40%. That's when I operate at my best—creating, problem-solving, and refining processes that set a business up for long-term success."

This approach helps hiring managers visualise where you fit into their company beyond just your experience—it gives them a sense of where you'll add the most value.

Final Thoughts: Career Alignment and Long-Term Success

The concept of flow isn't just about feeling good at work—it's about sustained career success and fulfilment. When you operate in a state of flow, you're naturally more productive, engaged, and likely to excel in your role. Employers notice this energy, and it leads to better opportunities, career growth, and long-term satisfaction.

By identifying the moments when work feels effortless, you gain clarity on where you should be focusing your job search, what questions to ask in interviews, and how to evaluate new opportunities.

So, ask yourself: what were you doing the last time work felt easy and enjoyable? What skills were you using? Who were you working with? What challenges excited you? Your answers to these questions hold the key to your next career move—one that doesn't just look good on paper but aligns with how you work best.

The future of hiring isn't about AI replacing recruiters or impersonal processes ruling the job market. It's about balance. Companies that invest in people, create thoughtful hiring processes, and prioritise culture and growth over quick placement wins will always attract and retain the best talent.

Continuous improvement isn't just a buzzword—it's the key to building a successful career, a thriving team, and a strong business. Whether you're hiring, job hunting, or working in recruitment, never stop evolving. The more effort we put into growth, the better outcomes we'll see in the long run.

If you've made it this far, thank you—for trusting me to guide you through this journey.

This book wasn't just about teaching interview techniques or decoding recruiter lingo. It was about reminding you of your worth, reigniting your confidence, and helping you take back control of your career story.

You now have the tools to stand out, ask better questions, present your value, and walk into any interview room with clarity and purpose.

Remember: interviews aren't just about being chosen—they're about choosing the right fit for you, too.

Keep refining, keep learning, and back yourself—because no one else can do what you do, the way you do it.

Here's to the next chapter in your story. You've got this.

Resources and Tools for Success
Practical Templates, Checklists, and Guidelines to Support Every Step of Your Job Search

Designed to complement the strategies and insights covered throughout this book, the following pages provide actionable templates, examples, and checklists to help you stay organised, confident, and professional at every stage of your job search.

Creating a Strong Résumé & Cover Letter

Your résumé and cover letter are often your first impression with an employer, so they need to be clear, well-organised, and tailored to the role. Remember, the person reviewing your résumé might not know your industry, so make your experience easy to grasp at a glance.

Résumé Tips
- List your availability for a call or interview at the top to make it easy for employers to contact you.

- Keep your résumé concise, ideally between two to five pages, with the most important details at the top.

- Use an Australian-friendly format, ensuring your résumé is well-structured, professional, and easy to read.

- Highlight transferable skills, particularly if you are new to the Australian job market or transitioning into a new industry.

- Include volunteering experience to demonstrate your work ethic and community involvement.

- Frame international experience in an Australian context by explaining responsibilities and achievements in a way that aligns with local job descriptions.

- Include certifications or courses completed in Australia to demonstrate your commitment to learning and adapting to the local job market. If you have qualifications from another country, mention them, but also check if they need to be formally recognised in Australia.

- Use clear section headings and bullet points to improve readability and ensure key information is easy to find.

- Avoid generic statements—use quantifiable achievements where possible, such as: "Managed a team of 10 staff and improved efficiency by 20% through new scheduling methods."

Pro Tip: If you have gaps in your employment history, consider explaining them in a positive way, such as highlighting skill-building activities, volunteer work, or further education.

Cover Letter Tips

Your cover letter is a chance to introduce yourself, express enthusiasm for the role, and explain how your experience and skills align with the job.

- Keep it to one page, tailored to the specific role and company.

- Start with a strong introduction that expresses your enthusiasm for the role and the company.

- Clearly state how you can contribute rather than just listing your qualifications. Employers want to know how you can make an impact.

- Research the company before writing and mention specific projects, values, or initiatives that resonate with you.

- Make it conversational yet professional, ensuring it doesn't feel like a generic template.

- Be honest about your experience while framing it in a way that highlights your strengths. If you are new to the Australian workforce, focus on skills like teamwork, adaptability, and problem-solving.

- End with a call to action, such as: "I look forward to discussing this opportunity further. I am available for a phone interview at your convenience."

Pro Tip: If English is not your first language, consider asking a mentor, career advisor, or friend to review your cover letter to ensure clarity and professionalism.

Dos and Don'ts for Job Applications

A strong application not only showcases your skills and experience but also reflects your professionalism and attention to detail. Avoiding common mistakes and following best practices can make a significant difference in your job search success.

Do's

- Customise your application for each role rather than sending a generic résumé and cover letter.

- Tell the employer how you can make an impact, rather than just explaining why you are a good fit for the role.

- Research the company and role before applying so you are prepared if contacted for an interview.

- Be honest about your experience and reasons for leaving previous roles (if necessary, briefly address employment gaps with a positive approach).

- Ask for feedback from friends, mentors, or career advisors on your résumé and job applications.

- Use clear formatting and keep the layout professional and easy to read.

- Include a call to action in your cover letter, outlining your availability for an interview.

- Keep track of the jobs you apply for so you can respond confidently if contacted.

- Check spelling and grammar in both your résumé and cover letter – in Australia, use UK English (e.g., "organisation" instead of "organization").

- Write a summary about yourself and your experience – this gives the reader an insight into your background.

Pro Tip: If you do not have professional Australian references, you can include references from volunteer work, community organisations, or training programs.

Don'ts

- Avoid repetition in your résumé and cover letter.

- Never lie about your experience—employers can verify details, and dishonesty can hurt future opportunities.

- Don't make it too long—résumés should be a maximum of five pages, and cover letters should be limited to one page.

- Don't forget a call to action—express your interest and availability.

- Don't forget to update your résumé regularly—every time you gain experience, complete a course, or learn new skills.

Interview Preparation Checklist

This checklist combines both practical and mindset-based steps to help you feel calm, clear, and confident on the day.

Research and Understanding
- I've researched the company's background, values, mission, and leadership team.
- I understand the role's responsibilities, who it reports to, and how it fits into the company.

Question Preparation
- I've prepared thoughtful questions to ask during the interview.
- I've considered asking questions like "What does success look like in the first 90 days?" or "How is performance measured?"

Presentation and Professionalism
- I've chosen an outfit that aligns with the company's dress code and culture.
- My appearance reflects a professional, polished presence.

Logistics and Essentials
- I've mapped out my route, accounted for traffic or delays, and planned to arrive early.
- I've packed multiple copies of my résumé, my cover letter, the job description, and any supporting documents.

Confidence and Delivery
- I've practised answers to common interview questions out loud, so I feel more natural saying them in the moment.
- I've prepared clear, relevant examples using the STAR method or another structured approach.
- I've checked my overall presence to ensure I'm coming across as engaged and confident—without overthinking it.

Wellbeing and Mindset
- I've had a good night's sleep, eaten well, and stayed hydrated.
- I've taken a moment to reflect on my strengths and remind myself that I deserve to be here.
- I feel mentally and emotionally prepared to show up as my best self in the interview.

Company Research Checklist

Use this checklist to guide your research and walk into your interview informed, aligned, and ready to connect.

Company Snapshot

- I've visited the company's website to understand its founding story, mission, vision, services, and values.

- I've reviewed the About Us section and noted key milestones or turning points in their journey.

Leadership Team

- I've explored the founder's and leadership team's profiles on LinkedIn.

- I fully understand their career paths, industry experience, and areas of expertise.

Recent News and Developments

- I've looked up recent media coverage, blog posts, or press announcements.

- I'm across any new projects, partnerships, or strategic moves.

Social Media Presence

- I've explored the company's activity on LinkedIn, Facebook, Instagram, or other platforms.

- I've noted the tone, content themes, and how they engage with their audience.

Client Base and Industry Position
- I've identified who the company serves and what industries they operate in.
- I'm aware of standout clients, their unique selling points, and major competitors.

Company Culture and Internal Communication
- I've looked for signs of internal celebrations, learning opportunities, flexibility, and values in action.
- I've reached out to mutual LinkedIn connections (if any) for insights.

Projects and Initiatives
- I've researched key projects or initiatives the company is currently working on.
- I'm ready to provide insights on projects or draw on previous experiences if asked.

Values and Causes
- I understand the company's mission, core values, and social or environmental causes they support.
- I've prepared questions about how these values are reflected in their day-to-day work.

Interviewer's Background
- I've viewed the LinkedIn profiles of my interviewer(s) or hiring manager.

- I've identified any shared interests, experiences, or mutual connections.

Organisational Structure
- I understand where the role I'm applying for fits within the business.
- I know who I would likely report to or work closely with.

Understanding the Market
- I know who their main competitors are and what challenges they may be facing.
- I understand their competitive advantages and market positioning.

Personal Reflection (Gut Check)
- I've reflected on whether this company aligns with my personal and professional goals.
- I can genuinely see myself working here, adding value, and growing with the business.

Solopreneur Research Checklist

Use this checklist when preparing for an interview with a solopreneur or founder-led business.

Solopreneur Snapshot
- I've reviewed their website, especially the About page and any blog content.
- I've researched their professional background and reputation.

Social Media Presence
- I've explored their tone, consistency, and how they engage with followers.
- I've noted any patterns in communication or presentation style.

Public Presence
- I've listened to interviews, podcasts, or videos they've been featured in.
- I've followed any client tags or online discussions mentioning their work.

Feedback and Testimonials
- I've checked for Google reviews, LinkedIn recommendations, or social proof.
- I've looked for testimonials that reflect on their leadership and communication.

Work Style and Professionalism
- I understand how they communicate expectations and boundaries.
- I've reflected on whether their working style feels clear and respectful.

Red Flags to Watch For
- Vague or changing role expectations
- No clear contract, job scope, or pay structure

LinkedIn Profile Tips

LinkedIn is one of your most powerful online tools. Whether you're actively job hunting or simply maintaining your professional presence, a strong profile helps you stay visible, connected, and credible. Recruiters who search for candidates often use keywords related to skills, systems, and job titles, so make sure your profile includes accurate and relevant information.

Essentials to Include

- **Profile Photo:** Use a clear, approachable photo—ideally in professional attire.

- **LinkedIn Banner:** Add a relevant, visually appealing banner to personalise your page.

- **Open to Work:** If you're actively job seeking, consider using the "Open to Work" feature.

- **Headline:** Go beyond your job title. Use a phrase that highlights your strengths (e.g. "Customer Service Specialist | Passionate about creating standout client experiences").

- **About Section:** Write in first person. Share your skills, what drives you, and the type of work you're seeking.

- **Experience:** List key responsibilities and achievements for each role.

- **Skills:** Include a mix of technical and soft skills. Keep them current.

- **Featured Section:** Showcase links to projects, your résumé, articles, or a short video introduction if you're comfortable on camera.

Pro Tips
- Engage with content in your industry—like, comment, and share thoughtfully to stay active and visible.

- Use LinkedIn to reach out for mentorship or informal chats—it's a networking platform, not just an online CV.

- Make sure your résumé and LinkedIn profile align in terms of titles, dates, and tone.

- If you're job searching discreetly, set your "Open to Work" preferences so only recruiters can see them.

Mastering Common Interview Questions

This section supports your confidence by helping you prepare for some of the most common and impactful questions interviewers ask. Your goal isn't to memorise answers—it's to know your stories, express your value clearly, and respond in a way that feels natural and authentic. The trick is in preparation, not perfection. Use real examples and speak to your strengths with clarity—not ego.

Strength-Based Questions
When talking about your strengths, think about:
- What do I enjoy doing?

- What do I do well without much guidance?

- What kind of feedback have I received?

Examples:
- I enjoy solving problems and making things more efficient. In my last role, I streamlined a system that saved the team hours each week.

- I'm often the go-to person for communicating with stakeholders. I've learned how to adjust my style depending on who I'm talking to, and it's helped me build strong working relationships.

Weakness Questions

Reframe the word "weakness" as "areas for improvement" and share how you've taken steps to address it.

Examples:
- I used to struggle with delegation but have since learned to trust others and give clearer instructions. It's helped my projects run more smoothly.

- Technical writing wasn't a strength for me early on, so I enrolled in a short course last year and now feel much more confident presenting my ideas in writing.

Popular Questions and Prompts

These are your interview warm-ups—designed to help the interviewer get to know you quickly, so make them count. Don't rush—pause, breathe, and remember that your goal is connection, not perfection.

- Tell me about yourself

- Why do you want to work here?

- What's your greatest achievement?

- Where do you see yourself in five years?

- Tell us about a time you worked in a team

- Describe a time you handled conflict

Sample Answers to Common Interview Questions
Tell me about yourself
Here are three ways to tailor this answer depending on your strengths:
Professional and Personal Balance
Outside of work, I enjoy reading fiction, going to the gym, and spending time with friends and family—especially trivia nights on Tuesdays. Professionally, I've spent over six years in the medical field and am passionate about growing within a company that values development. My coworkers describe me as diligent, punctual, and outcome-driven. Recently, I read 50 books in a year and received five customer commendations in a single month.

Highlighting Upbringing and Hobbies
I grew up by the beach, which sparked my love of surfing and fishing. I also play guitar and perform at a local pub with friends. My professional background is in hospitality, where I advanced to a team leader role. That experience sharpened my leadership, organisation, and customer service skills—qualities I'm eager to bring into this role.

Linking Personal Growth to Professional Goals
After moving to Australia five years ago, I've been focused on building experience in my field of study. I enjoy gardening, cooking, and family outings. This year, I'm completing a personal fitness challenge. Professionally,

I'm excited to apply my academic foundation and passion for innovation in a role where I can make a real impact.

Additional Common Questions and Sample Answers
Why do you want to work here?
I'm drawn to your focus on innovation and ethical leadership. A friend who works here shared how supported and encouraged they feel, which really stood out. I'd love to contribute to that kind of forward-thinking environment.

Why should we hire you?
I bring the right skills, industry experience, and a strong work ethic. I'm dedicated, quick to learn, and genuinely motivated to help your team succeed. While I'm confident in what I can contribute from day one, I'm also open to learning new systems, approaches, and ways of thinking that will help me grow within the role and add even more value over time.

What's your greatest achievement?
At my last job, I led a process improvement project that saved the team 10 hours each week. It was my first experience stepping into a leadership role, and it showed me the kind of impact I can make when I take initiative and trust my instincts.

Where do you see yourself in five years?
In five years, I hope to be in a leadership position—mentoring others while working on projects that challenge me both creatively and strategically. Ideally, I'll still be growing with a company like yours—one that values people, innovation, and progress.

Tell us about a time you worked in a team.
I worked on a high-pressure client campaign with a tight deadline. Everyone had different working styles, which created a bit of friction, so I suggested a short 10-minute daily huddle. It helped us align quickly, stay on

track, and ultimately deliver the project ahead of schedule.

Describe a time you dealt with conflict.

During a group project, one of my teammates kept missing deadlines. Rather than escalating it, I had a private conversation with them and learned they were struggling with part of the task. We reallocated the work and gave them the technical support they needed. It turned a potential conflict into a great example of collaboration.

What motivates you at work?

I'm motivated by variety and forward momentum. I enjoy solving problems, learning new things, and seeing results—whether that's a satisfied client, an improved system, or a successful project. Being part of a team that values impact, contribution, and collaboration keeps me energised.

What are you looking for in your next role?

I'm looking for a role where I can contribute meaningfully and continue developing professionally. A supportive team, clear goals, and opportunities to grow are really important to me. I'm especially motivated by environments where I can take initiative and help drive results.

Mastering Behavioural and Situational Questions

Behavioural and situational questions are designed to understand how you've handled past situations or how you would approach future ones. Below are example responses to help guide your preparation—remember to provide plenty of context when answering.

The STAR Method Refresher

Use this structure to guide your answers:

Situation – What was happening? What was the context?

Task – What were you responsible for?
Action – What did you do?
Result – What was the outcome?

Common Questions to Practise

- Can you describe a time when you faced a challenge and how you overcame it?

- Tell me about a time when you had to deal with a difficult customer or client.

- Describe a situation where you had to work under pressure.

- Give an example of a time you worked in a team to achieve a goal.

Sample Answers to Behavioural and Situational Questions
Overcoming a Challenge
A customer was upset about a delayed shipment. I listened to their concerns, apologised for the inconvenience, and offered a discount on their next purchase. The customer appreciated the gesture and continued shopping with us.

Working Under Pressure
During a peak season, I managed multiple deadlines by prioritising tasks, communicating clearly with my team, and staying focused. We delivered every project on time and received positive client feedback.

Achieving a Goal
I set a goal to increase my sales by 20% in six months. I studied new techniques, personalised my approach with clients, and followed up more consistently. I ended up exceeding my goal and was asked to train the next new hire.

Team Collaboration

For a product launch, I led the marketing side—collaborating with multiple teams and managing timelines. The campaign went live successfully, and sales outperformed targets.

Adapting to Change

When our company introduced new systems, I upskilled quickly and helped train others. This eased the transition and improved team productivity.

Resolving Conflict

I had a disagreement with a colleague over project priorities. I initiated a conversation, actively listened to their perspective, and we found a solution that satisfied both of us and moved the project forward.

Extended Example – Project Management

I was given full responsibility to design new processes aimed at improving customer experience, with a three-month deadline. I identified key gaps, developed clear staff tools and training resources, and consulted stakeholders throughout. Every deliverable was completed on time, and the changes led to improved customer feedback, streamlined onboarding, and better team efficiency. The project helped me grow as a manager and gave me the confidence to lead larger initiatives. Use these examples as inspiration, not scripts. The most memorable answers reflect your own values, voice, and real-life experience.

Asking Questions in an Interview

Asking thoughtful questions not only helps you assess whether a role is right for you, but also demonstrates initiative, curiosity, and professionalism. Below are examples of strong questions to ask both recruiters and hiring managers during the interview.

What to Ask a Recruiter

These questions help you gather context, understand expectations, and gain insight into the role and the company from the recruiter's perspective:

- What can you tell me about the company's culture and values?

- How did this role become available?

- What are the key challenges someone in this position might face?

- Do you have any tips for succeeding in the interview?

- Have you recruited for this role or company before? If so, what made previous candidates successful or unsuccessful?

- How does the company typically onboard new hires?

- What do you think the hiring manager values most in a candidate?

- What drew you to work with this client?

- Are there any potential hurdles I should be aware of—either during the interview process or in the role itself?

Pro Tip: Asking about past placements can be particularly insightful. For example:

"Have you recruited this role for the company before? If so, why didn't the previous placement work out?"

This kind of transparency gives you a clearer picture of the challenges and reveals how well the recruiter knows the business.

Questions to Ask in a Direct Interview

Tailor your questions depending on who you're speaking with, the level of the role, and the tone of the conversation. Here are some common themes and example questions:

Career Progression

- What does career progression look like for this role?

Learning About the Hiring Manager

- I noticed that [Hiring Manager's Name] has been with the company for a while. What drew you to this role, and what's kept you here?

Setting Expectations

- What would the first month or two in this role look like?

- What are the key objectives you'd like me to achieve during this time?

Measuring Success

- If this role has been filled previously, how was success measured?

- If this is a new role, how do you define success in the position?

Team Dynamics and Culture

- Can you tell me more about the team I'd be working with and how they collaborate?

- What's the broader company culture like?

History and Story (when interviewing with the owner)
- I've done some research on the business, but I'd love to hear more about how it all started.

Competitiveness and Next Steps
- May I ask how many candidates you're currently interviewing for this role?

- When are you hoping to fill the position, and what does the onboarding process involve?

90-Day Plan Checklist

Use this checklist to review, refine, and confidently present your 90-day plan during your second interview with the company.

Structure & Phasing
- I've structured my plan into clear 30, 60, and 90-day phases.
- Each phase has a distinct focus: onboarding, contribution, and impact.
- My plan flows logically and is easy to follow at a glance.

Role Alignment
- I've tailored the plan to the role I'm applying for (sales, operations, general, etc.).
- The goals and actions align with what success looks like in this position.
- I've considered the company's size, team structure, and pace when shaping the plan.
- The scope of my plan matches the level of the role (entry-level, mid-tier, leadership).

Business Awareness
- I've incorporated what I know about the company's values, goals, and culture.
- My plan reflects current industry trends or known business chal-

lenges.

- I've used language that mirrors how the company describes its work and priorities.

- I've factored in industry-specific needs (e.g. compliance, creativity, service, innovation).

Learning & Onboarding
- My first 30 days include learning about the business, tools, and understanding the culture and team dynamic.

- I've outlined how I'll gain product/service knowledge.

Contribution & Early Wins
- My 60-day phase outlines how I'll begin contributing meaningfully whilst also seeking feedback.

- I've included ideas for participating in or supporting projects and identified opportunities for small improvements or efficiencies.

- I've considered realistic deliverables based on the role's level of authority and influence.

- I've listed key people I'd aim to meet or build relationships with.

- I've included at least 2–3 tangible, achievable goals for this phase.

Strategy, Results & Forward Focus
- My 90-day phase includes a clear goal or outcome that demonstrates value.

- I've described how I'll refine my strategy based on early feedback.

- I've proposed future goals or next steps beyond the 90 days.
- I've suggested at least one improvement, innovation, or idea for the business.
- I've shown how these goals contribute to the broader team or business objectives.

Presentation & Communication
- I've prepared to position this as a draft, open to feedback.
- I've included a clean one-page version or visual breakdown (table or slide).
- I've rehearsed how to confidently talk through the plan in the interview.
- I've tied parts of my plan to real company priorities or challenges.
- I've made sure the tone reflects enthusiasm, curiosity, and professionalism.

Adaptability & Relevance
- I've made it clear that this plan is adaptable as I learn more.
- I've avoided making assumptions or sounding prescriptive.

The Interview Follow-Up Checklist and Templates

A thoughtful follow-up message reinforces your interest and leaves a lasting impression. Keep it short, sincere, and well-written—aim for 3 to 5 concise lines. Review spelling, grammar, and tone before hitting send. Templates can help, but they should always be tailored.

Follow-Up Essentials

- Use a professional subject line, such as "Thank You – [Your Name], Interview for [Job Title]" or "Following Up – [Your Name], Interview on [Date]"

- Clearly express your continued interest in the role—or politely withdraw if your situation has changed.

- If you've already sent a thank-you, wait at least a week before checking in again.

- Stay in touch, even if the role is filled or placed on hold. Good companies are always hiring, and a well-timed check-in keeps you front of mind.

- If you interviewed with multiple people, either include them all in the email or mention their names respectfully in your message.

Pro Tip: Avoid sending mass or copy-paste emails—this is where people often make mistakes, such as using the wrong name or referencing the wrong role. Be intentional, take your time, and send with care.

Follow-Up Interview Templates

Template 1: Standard Follow-Up After Interview

Subject: Thank You – [Your Name], Interview for [Job Title] on [Date]

Dear [Interviewer's Name],

Thank you for the opportunity to interview for the **[Job Title]** role at **[Company Name]** on **[Interview Date]**. I appreciated the chance to learn more about the team and the exciting work you're doing, particularly [mention a specific point discussed]. After our conversation, I remain enthusiastic about the opportunity to contribute [insert a key strength] and be part of an organisation that values [mention company value or mission].

I look forward to hearing about the next steps in the process.

Warm regards,

[Your Name]

Template 2: Follow-Up When You Haven't Heard Back

Subject: Following Up – [Your Name], Interview for [Job Title]

Dear [Interviewer's Name / Hiring Manager],

I hope this message finds you well. I wanted to follow up on our interview for the **[Job Title]** position on **[Date]**. I really enjoyed our conversation and learning more about the role and your team. I completely understand how busy things can get, but I just wanted to check in to see if there are any updates regarding the next steps. I remain very interested in the opportunity and would be grateful for any information you're able to share.

Warm regards,

[Your Name]

Template 3: Follow-Up After a Second Interview or Task

Subject: Thank You – [Your Name], Second Interview for [Job Title]

Dear [Interviewer's Name],

Thank you again for the opportunity to meet with you and the team for the second round of interviews. I appreciated the in-depth discussion and was particularly excited to learn more about [mention specific topic, project, or team member].

I'm looking forward to the possibility of contributing to **[Company Name]** and applying my experience in [insert relevant experience] to the **[Job Title]** role.

Please let me know if there's anything further you need from me.

Warm regards,

[Your Name]

Template 4: Declining the Role Politely

Subject: Thank You for the Opportunity – [Your Name]

Dear [Interviewer's Name / Hiring Manager],

Thank you for taking the time to meet with me about the **[Job Title]** position. I appreciated the opportunity to learn more about the role and your team.

After careful consideration, I have decided to withdraw my application, as I believe another opportunity is better aligned with my goals at this time. I'm genuinely grateful for your time and the professional manner in which the process was conducted.

I hope our paths cross again in the future and wish you and your team continued success.

Kind regards,

[Your Name]

Final Thoughts: From Preparation to Confidence

This chapter is about giving you tools to step into every opportunity prepared, aligned, and confident. You don't have to use every checklist or follow every script word-for-word. What matters is that you've taken the time to understand what works for you—and that you're now equipped to show up with intention.

Whether you're refining your résumé, preparing for a second interview, or reaching out to a recruiter, let these tools be your safety net and your springboard. You've got more control than you think—and every time you prepare with purpose, you build the kind of quiet confidence that employers notice.

Afterword

This book was never just about job interviews. It's about backing yourself, finding clarity in the chaos, and knowing how to show up as *you*—fully and confidently.

I've sat across from thousands of people—nervous, excited, second-guessing themselves, hoping to be seen. Regardless of experience level, the insecurities are often the same. *How do I stand out? How do I sell myself? How do I explain leaving my last role?*

The answer is already within you—it just needs to be unlocked. Authenticity, purpose, and passion drive all of us. And if you haven't quite found your path yet, don't worry—it's there.

Writing this was my way of pulling together everything I've learned. Not just to help people "get the job," but to help them *understand their value*, *trust their voice*, and *stand out for the right reasons*.

If this book helped you feel a little more confident, a little more prepared—or simply reminded you that you've got what it takes—then it's done what I hoped it would.

If you found value in this book, please consider leaving a review on Amazon or Goodreads. Your feedback helps others discover helpful resources for their own career journey.

Thank you for your support.

—Tanya Abbey

About the Author

With over 20 years of experience in recruitment, sales, and business management, Tan is a passionate professional dedicated to connecting people, driving business growth, and fostering meaningful relationships. Her career is built on authenticity, openness, and a commitment to delivering real, tangible results for clients, candidates, and business partners.

As the founder of RecruitCorpGroup, Tan has supported businesses of all sizes—locally, nationally, and internationally—to streamline operations, build strong teams, and achieve sustainable growth. She is a generalist recruiter, having recruited across every industry and level, from entry-level roles to executive leadership, in both Australian and global markets.

Her expertise spans workforce development, recruitment strategy, small business consulting, and employer branding, making her a sought-after advisor for companies, government initiatives, and not-for-profits alike.

Tan is also a Small Business Mentor with the Queensland Government, working closely with founders and growing teams to scale sustainably, and a Career Mentor with Headspace, supporting young people in building confidence, employability, and purpose. She regularly delivers recruitment and business workshops for small businesses, community organisations, and career programs—equipping others with the tools to hire well, grow confidently, and lead with heart.

Over the years, she has conducted more than 15,000 interviews and placed over 5,000 candidates. Known for her "old-school" 360-degree recruitment style, she brings a relationship-first, strategic approach to every hire and every business conversation.

Tan also works alongside support organisations and community programs to deliver employment workshops, mentoring, and real-world tools for people at every stage of their career. As part of her commitment to meaningful impact, 30% of profits from her book will be donated to the Romero Centre for the first three months of launch, supporting employment access and career empowerment for people seeking safety and opportunity in Australia.

This book—written over 12 months and independently published—is her first self-published work. It's more than just a guide; it's a reflection of her lived experience, lessons from the field, and belief that everyone deserves the tools to show up and succeed.

First and foremost, Tan is a proud mum of two boys as well as a lifelong Queensland Maroons supporter, and co-host of the Quick Hands Rugby League Podcast. She values community, integrity, and collaboration—and is always up for a good book, a bit of banter, or a meaningful conversation.

Also by Tanya Abbey

Finding Work, Building Futures
A Practical Guide for Refugees and People Seeking Asylum
Available on Amazon

Coming Soon by Tanya Abbey

Hire Humans, Not résumés
A Small Business Book to Building People-First Teams
Keys to the Castle
Unlocking Growth While Keeping the Basement Locked
Stay Connected
If you found value in this book, I'd love to stay in touch. Follow me for updates on new releases, bonus resources, workshops, and tools to support your next steps.
LinkedIn
https://www.linkedin.com/in/tabbey
Instagram
https://www.instagram.com/tanya.abbey

www.ingramcontent.com/pod-product-compliance
Lightning Source LLC
Chambersburg PA
CBHW061726070526
44583CB00024B/3026